TRULY GROUNDED

TRULY GROUNDED

Insights For The Seasons Of Life

Evelyn Holt-Fuller

Truly Grounded: Insights For The Seasons Of Life
Copyright © 2024, by Evelyn Holt-Fuller

ISBN: 979-8-218-54987-9

Published by ESE Media
Printed in the United States of America

DEDICATION

To my son, **Eric D. Fuller**, thank you for the story you shared with me. All my love to you, my "offsprout."

ACKNOWLEDGEMENTS

With deep appreciation I acknowledge the following people for their valuable assistance, kindness, and support: **Clementine Clark, Anita Daniels, Dana Hensley, Jamila Holt, Edith Isler, Christopher Lynch, Dr. Prince R. Rivers, Dr. Dawn Samad, Angela Taylor, Gail Taylor, and Meyerstine Tookes.**

To **Janice and Carolyn**, the best sisters-in-law anyone could ever hope to have. You both are wonderful blessings.

A very special thank-you to **Penda L. James**, Scribe Coach, for her enthusiasm, encouragement and prayers. Her insight, knowledge, and input increased my understanding of the publishing process exponentially. She kept encouraging me and helping me until I finished this project. Like that one, lone leaf that holds on to the tip of a limb all through the winter, she stuck by me and saw me through *my* "winter" of confusion, not knowing where to turn. I'm very grateful for her unwavering support and dedication.

Introduction

I don't want to leave this world without having impacted it in some way.

Do our stages of life, what we call our "seasons," end, or do they simply cycle? "Cycling," can be defined as *continual* growth and development, and as we cycle through the seasons of life, we gain knowledge, wisdom and insight about ourselves and how we all relate to each other.

Truly Grounded: Insights for the Seasons of Life reminds us that, even though some growth experiences may be unpleasant, they serve to make us stronger, more resilient, and more resourceful. They help us realize that we can withstand *and* survive the chaos, confusion and craziness of the world.

Truly Grounded is provocative, straightforward, and authentic. It is also multi-genre and commentary based. Some narratives address complex social issues, while others are simply my thoughts and opinions about society. Still others challenge us to look at commonplace things and view them from a totally different, and deeply philosophical perspective.

Truly Grounded also has a lighter side. Within some of the serious narratives, bits of wit, humor, and satire emerge to lighten the mood. These little tidbits invite readers to smile, chuckle, or even laugh out loud.

Ultimately, *Truly Grounded* celebrates our ability to learn from the past, embrace the present, and look to the future. When we are truly grounded, no matter what life throws at us, we rise up, we keep the faith, we keep moving forward.

Contents

PART I: RELATABLES

Even though we're all different, we sometimes share common experiences, things that we all can relate to. For example, if I said, "rickety shopping cart," without saying anything else, you'd know, immediately, exactly what I'm talking about because we've all experienced that cart with the wobbly wheel. It's those shared experiences – how we relate to each other in our mutual understanding of common things – that is the theme of "Relatables."

You've Been Randomly Chosen To Receive...

How do you handle unsolicited phone calls from unknown companies? What do you say when they ask you to send money?

Thanks to my wise, ninety-three-year-old Uncle Henry, I know exactly how to avoid scammers. Uncle Henry said, "I figure, if anyone really has money for me, they'd just send it. Why call me to tell me they're going to send it? They can send it by registered mail, too."

Several years ago, before smartphones, while sitting in my car waiting for a friend to come out of the doctor's office, I answered a call from an unknown number. Fortunately for me (and unfortunately for him), I was in a particularly playful mood that day, and when I'm in those moods, I like to (bleep), uhhh "play" with people for the fun of it.

"I have a $100 gas card for you," said the guy on the other end of the line. "All you have to do is send us a $4.95 processing fee."

Slyly I said, "Oh, I don't have $4.95," but he quickly followed with, "Oh, well, just give me your checking account number and we can deduct it." I replied, "Oh nooooo. I don't give out my checking information to anyone." Undeterred, he popped back with, "Well what about a credit card? We need to get the processing fee before we can send you your $100 gas card."

A devilish grin etched across my face as I presented him with my coups de grâce. "Okay. I've got a better idea." I could almost feel his intense excitement. No doubt he thought I had fallen for his spiel. Barely able to keep from laughing, I said, "Why don't you just take the $4.95 processing fee out of the $100 and send me the $95.05 balance? With that, he hung up.

Sadly, those kinds of scams are becoming more common these days. What's even worse is that some people fall for them. With all the information out there to help us, why do we still trust people who call us out of the blue? Certainly, we don't want to become a country of skeptics, but sometimes it pays not to be so trusting. Even the federal government warns us to be wary when someone initiates a call. It's one thing if you call them, but if a company calls you out of the blue, run!

I'm No Thomas Payne, But I'm Just Sayin'

— Why does it take me two weeks to lose the five pounds that jumped on me overnight? I'm just sayin'.
— Of all the carts in the store, why does the one you get always have a broken wheel? I'm just sayin'.
— For years you pay hundreds of dollars a month for insurance. Then when you use it, your premiums go up or they cancel your policy. They should stop calling it an "insurance policy" and start calling it a "pay-not-to-use-it" policy. I'm just sayin'.
— Instead of trying to run away from death, think of it as your get-out-of-jail-free card. I'm just sayin'.
— If manufacturers spend less money by reducing the amount of salt and sugar in their products, or by removing preservatives, why do they charge us more? I'm just sayin'.
— If an entree comes with two sides, as pictured on the menu, why does the restaurant charge extra to substitute one of the sides? I'm just sayin'. Doesn't lettuce cost less than a potato? So why can't I have a salad instead of a potato? I'm just sayin'.
— Does anyone else feel the same as I, that restaurants shouldn't run out of any food item on the menu? I'm just sayin'.
— If all you ordered was a hamburger, no onions, and extra ketchup, and if the cashier asked you – at least three times – to repeat your order so they could verify it, why do you find your order messed up when you get home? I'm just sayin'.

— Why can't Mr. Murphy work his law on someone
else sometime? I'm just sayin'.
— Why do things go wrong just when you're next in
the checkout line? (The person in front of you has a
price check, or the cash register paper runs out or
malfunctions, or the clerk has to void an item, or . .
.) I'm just sayin'.
— Why is God your *co*-pilot? Isn't a co-pilot the one
who assists and supports the captain-in-command?
So if God is your co-pilot, who is the captain? You?
I think not! We are not qualified to fly the "aircraft"
of our lives. Left alone, we'd stray off course, lose
the flight pattern and wind up off the radar. We'd
neglect to monitor our instruments and systems
(i.e., our bodies) and end up in a wreck. Given all
this, shouldn't God be the *pilot*, not the *co*-pilot?
I'm just sayin'.
— Just because you don't believe in God doesn't mean
that God doesn't exist. I'm just sayin'. Do you
really think that your *dis*belief in God makes God
not exist? I'm just sayin'. The same is true of Jesus.
Just because you don't believe in Jesus as Savior
doesn't mean that He isn't. Jesus still died to give
us eternal life even if you don't believe. I'm just
sayin'.
— If the Scriptures tell us to respect and love
everyone; and God is not a respecter of people; and
all are one in Christ Jesus; then why did so many
"Christian" schools suddenly pop up after
intergration in the 1960s? I'm just sayin'.
— Every time you complain about getting older,
remind yourself of the alternative. I'm just sayin'.

— A new funeral home moved into the area. In their effort to attract business, the owners put a sign out front that read, "10% discount for first-time customers." Isn't every corpse a "first-time" customer (and last time one for that matter)? I'm just sayin'.

— If a company is offering you a 30-day free trial, shouldn't you be allowed to give them your credit card number *after* the thirty days, rather than up front? I'm just sayin'.

— Have you ever thought about this? You can get so wrapped up in a project that you go *all* day without eating or even thinking about food, but if you try going without food for a medical procedure or religious fast, all you can think about is eating. I'm just sayin'.

— Do you find it funny that medicine commercials warn you not to take the medicine if you are allergic to it or its ingredients? How will you know you're allergic if you don't take it? I'm just sayin'. And if you take it and then find out you're allergic to it, isn't it too late? I'm just sayin'.

— I asked myself, "Why pray for help to lose weight if you keep eating a big plate of food every time it passes in front of you?" I'm just sayin'.

— Why are there five people on a work crew if only one is working? I'm just sayin'.

— At the drive-thru, their only job is to put a straw, some napkins, and condiments in a bag and hand it to me. Why, then, when you get home, something is missing from my order? I'm just sayin'.

— Hat's off to all those manufacturers who make pre-
packaged meals, especially those that make cake-
in-a-box. It's a puzzle how they give you a little
bag of pre-mixed flour, and all you have to do is
add a couple of eggs, some oil and water, and you
end up with a whole two-layer cake that tastes
delicious. Yet when you bake one from scratch, and
use your best ingredients, hard work (and
sometimes even your prayers), it's still a hit or miss
whether it will turn out right.

— To those non-feminine, same-gender-loving
women, I get it. I understand why you're not a
femme, but what I don't get is why you imitate the
sloppy, pant-sagging boys. Why not imitate the
neatly dressed males? I'm just sayin'.

— If people are willing to stand in 96° heat or 20°
cold, holding up a "Need Help" sign, why can't
they hold up a stop sign on a work crew for $10 an
hour. I'm just sayin'. Or, why not ask a merchant
to pay them a few dollars a day to sweep the
sidewalk or pick up trash in front of their store? I'm
just sayin'.

— How can someone be homeless and hungry,
begging on the street, yet be smoking cigarettes,
drinking a beer, talking on a cell phone and feeding
a dog (or two)? I'm just sayin'.

— If you're using your outside voice while inside,
don't blame me if I turn to listen. I'm just sayin'.

— The person who always begins a task with the
phrase "I'm about to," or "I'm going to," never gets
the task done. I'm just sayin'.

— If I'm ever in a car accident, I have three prayers:

1. I pray that no one gets hurt.

2. I pray that I'm not at fault.

3. And for Heaven's sake, let the other driver be insured! I'm just sayin'.

— Thank you, thousands of mask wearers, for keeping us safe from *chin* COVID. I'm just sayin'.

— Since COVID, everyone has been super hyper-vigilent. We sanitize everything and wipe down every surface with bleach, alcohol, and every other disenfectant we can find. It kinda makes you wonder how many germs we ingested, touched or inhaled prior to COVID. I'm just sayin'.

— Who said "new math" was better? What's wrong with "old math"? 1+1 is still 2, no matter how you fancy it up. I'm just sayin'.

— What's wrong with rote learning? I'm just sayin'. I understand that we want our children to be critical and analytical thinkers, as well as problem-solvers, but the things we learned in elementary school via rote learning haven't change the answers. Plus, the facts that we learned through rote learning still stick with us 70-100 years later. In third grade, we learned our multiplication tables (which we called "times tables") all the way up to 12x12 = 144. And for anything past 12x12, we knew how to double- and triple-digit multiply. Seventy-plus years later, I still know that 1x1 = 1, 2x2 = 4, 4x4 =16, and so on. Figures don't change just because someone invented a new way to calculate them. We old folks can do math in our heads, without the use of a calculator, paper, or counting on fingers. Again, that was in third grade. *Third* grade. So I ask again, what's wrong with rote learning? I'm just sayin'.

— A friend of mine used to say that if a worldwide, catastrophic event happened, old folks would survive because we know how to make a fire with wood; grow, harvest, and preserve food; tell time on timepieces with hands; measure things without the use of electronics; use herbs for medicine; clean our bodies and clothes without running water; make clothes; be content without electricity, etc., etc. I'm just sayin'.

— The election is over. Your candidate either won or lost. Now come back and get all your campaign signs that are littering the roadsides. I'm just sayin'.

The Joneses: Who's Watching Whom?

Hey, Jonses. About our year-old cars? Time to trade.
But wait. I'm still paying off the first loan I made.
It's hard keeping up with you, so give me a break,
Please, please, please, for my pocketbook's sake.

What's that? You didn't tell me to copy you?
Yes, but what else am I going to do?
Is it jealousy, envy, or just my need for validation?
Seeking your approval just helps me function.

You have everything that I want and more,
When you shop, looks like you buy out the store.
So I copy you and shop like I have nothing to lose,
But if I keep this up I can't afford a pair of shoes.

Oh, dear Joneses, I'm not trying to be mean,
But being like you raises my self-esteem,
Until I take a sober look at the stuff I've bought,
Then I fall into depression; my self-esteem is shot.

Equipment, paintings, jewelry, airline tickets too,
Couldn't afford it but I wanted to be just like you.
Now I'm in debt up to my eyeballs
Just so I can say that I have as much as you all.

My house is full, attic and garage too,
Wall-to-wall with some things I'll never use.
Was it all worth it? Well for a while I say, "Yes."
I could gloat and say, "I'm just like the Joneses."

What? You didn't ask anyone to make you "king?"
Being "the Joneses" isn't really your thing?
Did "they" just draw the name "Jones" from a hat?
And say, "That name's ok; we'll just go with that."

You say nobody asked to borrow your name
To be the represenative of fortune and fame?
They didn't ask your permission to start a trend,
And make you the ones everyone wants to befriend?

Did you even know they would make up a slogan,
That "Keeping up with the Joneses" would be the one?
And when people say, "I want to be just like that,"
Does knowing that they copy you make you sad?

Oh, dear Joneses, it must be hard to bear the load
Of an unofficial title that you never chose.
To be viewed with delight, sometimes with disdain,
All because of your common last name.

All you did was go about your life as usual.
Then someone got the idea to put you on a pedestal.
I get you Joneses; just regular people buying things,
And it's people like me who start freaking.

We think you're rich; we think you're cool
Just because you own a beautiful swimming pool.
We imagine your stocks and bonds tucked in a safe,
Or hidden in a wall of some grand estate.

Oh? What's that? You're not really rich at all?
And you're not all that "on the ball?"

All that stuff you buy, all the bling and the glam;
You can't afford it either; it's just a sham.

To me you're a guiding light of the neighborhood.
Your success is undaunting, and well understood.
You say you see me always buying and shopping too?
Of course. 'Cause I'm trying to be like you.

Wait! What!? It's *my* house *you're* carefully watching?
Constantly seeing me buying and restocking.
A twist! What I think of you, you think the same of *me,*
Because *I'm* the Jones *you're* trying to be!?

Poof! Housework Be Gone!

Do you like housework? Well, I don't, but my sister does. Growing up, cooking was my thing and cleaning was hers. She couldn't boil water and I hid dirt to keep from having to deal with it.

To this day, when I happen to be in discussion with anyone about housework, they ask me, "Evelyn, what is your least favorite household chore? What's the one thing you disliked more than any other?" My answer, without hesitation, and with as many absolute adjectives that I can find, is this: "The absolute, number one chore that I definitely dislike about housework is *housework*."

Yep. Every time I think about picking up a broom, or pushing a mop, or dusting furniture, I try to find anything else to do but that. Unfortunately, (or fortunately), since I like a spotless house, doing household chores is a necessary evil.

You may be thinking to yourself, "If she hates housework that much, why doesn't she just hire a cleaning service?" Well, I have three reasons: First, I don't believe in forking over money for something that I can do by myself with very little effort. I only have four little rooms in my townhome and it takes literally 20-25 minutes for me to do a routine cleaning (40, if I mop.) Second, I don't trust anyone to clean as well as I do. Third, I don't want strangers traipsing all over my house.

One day, while trying to talk myself into getting up and cleaning my house, the thought came to me, "Do you *really* dislike all housework or just parts of it?" So, being the inquisitive person that I am, I decided to find out. Just for fun (or perhaps to prolong the inevitable), I constructed a very simple test. In one column, I listed all my usual household chores. Then, I put an "X" next to the ones that I truly disliked. Then, I put "OK" next to the ones I didn't mind so much. I fully expected all Xes, but what I got surprised me:

Sweeping	X
Vacuuming	X (I have no carpet, but I still don't like vacuuming)
Dusting	X (I use a Swiffer, but still don't like dusting.)
Washing Dishes	X (even though I live alone and usually only mess up 2-4 utensils)
Putting Dishes Away	X (I dislike this worse than washing them.)
Cleaning the Tub	X (at the top of my list of dislikes)
Doing Laundry	OK (but only the washing part)
Folding Clothes & Putting Them Away	X
Cleaning the Commode	OK (AND sanitizing it! Do you find this odd?)
Emptying Trash	OK
Cooking	OK

Making the Bed	OK (as long as I don't have to do anything fancy like tucking the spread under pillows, fluffing shams (which I don't have anyway), or placing decorative pillows (which I don't own) all over the bed. My friends tell me that I'm not truly making up the bed unless I do all that.)

Hmmm. I never expected an almost 50/50 split. I guess I'll have to change my tune about housework. Nottt!

In This Corner: Meds. And In The Other Corner: Side Effects

I've had the same wonderful doctor for years. We have a very good rapport with each other and I trust her medical knowledge and interest in keeping me healthy. I appreciate that she practices patient autonomy and informed consent.

A couple of years ago, when my cholesterol number crept up a few points, my doctor suggested that I consider taking a certain cholesterol-lowering drug (its name withheld here). I say "suggested" and "consider" because she knows that I don't like taking medications in the first place. Since my cholesterol wasn't at the top of the scale, I chose to start eating healthier and getting more exercise as an alternative to taking medications. Nonetheless, I was curious about the drug – a very popular one, prescribed by many doctors – so I researched it. The main reason for my research is that I'm always curious about the side effects of *any* medication that I take, and I usually try to find one with the fewest side effects. Do you agree that the "cure" shouldn't be worse than the ailment itself?

Screeeeeech! (That's me coming to a screeching halt, y'all, so I don't get in trouble.) Just so you don't get the wrong impression, I'm not telling anyone to *refuse* to take, or to *stop* taking any doctor-prescribed medication. If your doctor says you absolutely need a certain medication, take it. I myself take medications, and I also take vitamins and follow a health(ier) diet. I'm only suggesting that you research the suggested medication and discuss with your doctor the possibility of better alternatives, if there are any.

Certainly, we don't blame our doctors for trying to provide the best care, but do you agree that sometimes we need to be proactive and understand what we put in our bodies? As it turns out, this particular medication had many side effects.

Before even getting to that list of side effects, the manufacturer's first instructions read, "Eat low-fat, low-cholesterol foods." Well hells bells, Mr. Manufacturer! If we reduce fatty, cholesterol-filled foods, why would we need your drug? I'm just sayin'.

After that statement came a (lonnnng) list of side effects, beginning with those the company listed as *minor*: diarrhea, heartburn, gas, joint pain. (For those of us who already have arthritis, do we really want more joint pain?) The list continued with forgetfulness or confusion memory loss. (I'm almost eighty. Do I *really* want to speed up forgetfulness?)

But wait. We haven't gotten to the main list yet. The next statement read, "Some side effects can be serious. The following symptoms are uncommon, but if you experience any of them, call your doctor." (What?! Call the doctor if you think you're having serious side effects?! What, and wait for a callback?! Even if your doctor usually answers within a few hours, would you want to wait?) This line was followed by the phrase, "or get emergency medical help immediately." Ha! Say it with me, Ha! Do you think we're crazy, Mr. M.! Do you *really* think you need to tell us that?

Next came the company's list of "rare" and "uncommon" side effects. The list was too long to print here (over 30 in number), but I'll give you a few of them: muscle pain, tenderness, or weakness, lack of energy, loss of appetite (the only side effect we welcome, right?). The list continues: pain in the upper right part of the stomach (there only?), dark colored urine (oh my!), rash, hives, itching, hoarseness, and flu-like symptoms. (Flu-like symptoms!? You mean the same symptoms that could mean anything from a bad cold, to the actual flu, to COVID, pneumonia, or RSV?) Last came "yellowing of the skin or eyes." (Believe me, if my skin changes from black to yellow, you *definitely* don't have to tell me to seek emergency medical attention.)

At the end of the day, we still trust our doctors, especially those who believe in patient autonomy and informed consent, and those who aren't offended that we research things. Aren't you glad you live in this 21st Century world where knowledge is a few clicks away?

Rudeness and Inconsideration. Yes, I'm Fussing

Do you agree that we all could exhibit a little kindness and consideration toward others? One of my pet peeves is when people outright disregard others, their rights, and their feelings. Am I alone, or do you have some pet peeves too?

Loud Music. Yes, people have a right to play their music loud, but as the saying goes, "Your rights end where another person's rights begin." It's rude for people to bombard everyone else with their music. Do you agree that if they want to play it loud, they should put on some earbuds?!

Loud Talking, Especially in Closed Spaces. Why do people talk so loudly when they're inside, especially if the person they are talking to is right next to them? It's like they never heard of using their "inside voice?"

Cellphones on Speaker When in Public. Don't get mad at me if I listen to your conversation when you have your phone on speaker. Your conversation is no longer private.

Parking Over The Line. Do you agree that if a person thinks their vehicle is too precious to park properly, then they should leave it at home in the garage? It's rude to take up two spaces. Also, for those who find it difficult to pull into a space, maybe they need to go somewhere and practice and then come back and join the rest of us, right?

Parking In The "No Parking," Yellow Lines In Front Of Stores. No, you won't be "back in a second." No, you're not going to "run in the store just for a minute." You are creating a hazard by parking in front of the store. People have to get in the lane of oncoming traffic to go around you. Customers coming out of the store could get hit by passing vehicles because they can't see around yours.

Littering. If people don't want their trash, why do they think Mother Earth wants it? Why do they think someone else ought to pick up their garbage? Would they want to pick up someone else's garbage? And no, it's not job security. It's just plain rude.

Handicap Spaces. My number one pet peeve is any vehicle parked illegally in a handicap space. People who are not physically handicapped, should not park in that space. That includes people who borrow grandma's placard, or use grandma's car that has a sticker in it. It also includes the following: people who transport handicapped people but use the placard when *not* transporting them; people who forge stickers; and any other use by people who are not handicapped. Illegally using a handicap space has special significance to me because I did it once and it taught me a lesson that I will never forget. Here's what happened.

Back in the seventies, when I worked at a prominent university, part of my job was to make copies for my department, but our copy center happened to be across campus, in a small lot behind the library. Parking was very limited there. In addition, the lot was strictly enforced by security patrol. Being the self-serving, unempathetic person that I was at the time, it didn't bother me to break a few "innocent" rules now and then.

On this particular morning, after driving around for ten minutes, waiting for a space to open up, I darted into the only space left . . . a handicap space. "It'll only take me a few minutes to drop these papers off," I thought to myself.

I was halfway across the parking lot when I heard a voice calling out, "Ma'am! Ma'am! Can you tell me why you parked in my space?!" I turned to see a crippled man struggling to stand up as he exited his car. However, being the crude, self-absorbed person that I was back then, despite seeing him struggle, I still protested, "But I'll only be in here a minute. Just give me a minute." He didn't respond, but his demeanor gave me a hint that he was looking for a security guard. So I ran back to my car, hopped in, and began to back out of the spot. Only then did I read the handicap sign thoroughly. When he said it was his space, it really was *his* space. The university had assigned him a numbered space and erected a handicap sign that matched his handicap license plate. Mortified and convicted, I apologized profusely, and moved my car to a yellow-striped, "No Parking" area, preferring to take my chances there rather than keep this man from his space. Since that day, I've *never* parked in a handicap space for *any* reason.

Wait! I Need Help Losing Weight

I keep trying to lose weight but it always manages to find me. Why does it take two weeks to lose the five pounds that jumped on you overnight? What should you do? Join a weight-loss program, go on a diet, have surgery?

Sure, all the weight loss plans work fine for somebody, somewhere. Then again, it's hard for any program to work if you don't follow it, right?

I'm not a fan of taking pills, potions, and having surgeries. What about you?

That's only the tip of the iceberg for me. My problems are even bigger than that. I'm so skeptical of everything out there that I talk myself out of using any program before I even try it.

Mail order food kits? A great plan for those who like them. So how do I talk myself out of them? Well, I feel it's a waste of my money for any number of reasons. First, instead of carefully eating one little tray per meal, my lack of willpower would probably pull me into eating two of them at one sitting, then still go out and get a hamburger. Second, I figure why pay someone else to go out and buy foods for me, pack them in a box and have them shipped to me, when I could just walk across the street to my local grocery store and get the same food for myself?

Aside from healthy meal plans, some people try diet pills. Another good idea I guess, if that's what you want. But I talk myself out of that, too. Why? Well, if you read the fine print on the bottom of a diet pill box (or look closely at the writing on the bottom of the television screen), you see the words, "works best with proper diet and exercise." Well, jumpin' Jehoshaphat! *Any* diet program works if you eat right and exercise, don't you agree?!

Losing weight is good and healthy when done in a prescribed, practical way. Doctors always tell us that the best way to lose weight is to eat less, eat healthier, and exercise. My cousin tried it and he lost over sixty pounds in less than a year. (I hear you thinking, "A year!? That long!?" Yes. Patience is the key to losing weight and keeping it off.) Here's what he did:

1. He bought a few small plates, not much larger than a saucer.
2. He visualized the plate being divided into three sections, two small ones and one larger one. (A baby's food dish will do equally as well.)
3. He put a little meat, chicken or fish in one of the smaller compartments, fruit in the other, and filled the larger compartment with green vegetables. As an alternative, he sometimes substituted a starchy vegetable for the fruit.
4. He drank plenty of water, at least 2 quarts a day. Sometimes he put lemon juice or a cucumber slice in the water.
5. He cut way back on salt (especially never adding it to already cooked food) and used sugar substitutes.

Can we agree that whether you use a meal plan, exercise, eating less, or surgery, we should choose what

suits you? Maybe we can all encourage each other
along the way?

It Only Takes One

Have you ever been to a pig pickin'? I mean a real, old fashioned pig pickin' where they roast a whole hog on a spit, or in a pit, all night long and most of the next day. Finally, when it's ready, everyone gathers around and pulls some of that succulent, moist meat from the bones? If you've ever been to *that* kind of pig pickin', then you know the anticipation of waiting for that first bite of tender, juicy "oink-oink."

If you've never experienced that type of pig pickin', then how about a family reunion, a picnic in the park, or just a barbeque/cookout in the backyard? Just thinking about it makes your mouth water, huh?

Whatever the event, have you noticed that there's always one, uninvited guest that shows up to annoy you? No, I'm not talking about your crazy, drunk uncle or your loud, obnoxious cousin. They're easy to get rid of. I'm talking about those annoying little insects that seem to derive pleasure from tormenting you whenever you're outside trying to enjoy yourself.

If ants are the first things that come to mind, think again. Yes, ants are bothersome, but if you stop to think about it, ants don't care about you or what you're doing. They're too busy grabbing a few crumbs of bread to take back to their little anthill homes to stock up for winter.

If you're thinking bees, we're still not on the same page. Once you swat at a bee real good, he usually loses interest and goes on about his business.

I hear you thinking, "Is she gonna go through every insect on the planet until we guess the right one?" No,

I'm not doing that, so I'll just cut to the chase. To me, the most annoying, uninvited guests are flies and mosquitos, and to be clear, it's not a swarm of them, or even three or four. It's that *one* renegade that seems to be on a personal vendetta to wreak havoc in your life. There's always that *one* fly that keeps messing with you as if you said something about its mama. All the other flies are minding their own business, swarming over a chicken leg that somebody dropped on the ground, but not that *one* defector that seems hellbent on irritating you.

You know how it is. Your stomach's been growling for hours because you skipped breakfast to "save yourself" for this big meal. Then finally, after waiting in line for fifteen minutes, you reach the barbeque pit (or spit, or trough). Ummmm. A whiff of hickory floats past your nostrils, followed by the tantilizing aroma of sweet, Western North Carolina barbeque sauce. You load your plate with a big pile of barbeque, smother it in sauce, then scoop up big spoonfuls of potato salad and baked beans. Oh, and don't forget the slaw. Mama said you should always eat your veggies, right? If there's macaroni and cheese on the table, you plop some of that on there too. (It's a cookout, after all. Three starches are permitted.) For your coup de grâce, you lay on a couple of hushpuppies and a slice of sweet potato pie. Umm-mmm, your royal feast is ready! Now all you need is a throne to sit on. Ahhh, and there it is, a lawn chair that someone set out hair under the boughs of granny's grand oak tree. You sit down, carefully placing your plate in your lap and your tall glass of tea (or lemonade) in the cupholder. Now to reward yourself for holding out until this very moment.

Since you like a mingling of flavors, you scoop up little nibbles of each food, imagining your taste buds singing for joy as they savor each distinguishing flavor. "Ummmm." Your mind sings its enticing refrain, sending your imagination into frenzied anticipation. Your mouth waters ever so slightly, as it readies itself for your culinary delight.

Just when that first forkful is a mere centimeters from your waiting lips, here he comes, that dastardly, disgusting creature with oversized eyeballs that we call a fly! (I don't know why we always call flies and other insects "he," but we just do.) Before you can stop him, the incessant little creature lands smack dab on the edge of your plate. "Whyyyyyyy!" you scream inside your head. "Why me?! Why right now?!"

Now some flies come directly after your food, without hesitation. Maybe they're the youthful, foolhearty ones who throw caution to the wind and dive right in. But not that *one* seasoned, renegade. He likes to play little fly games. Oh, you've seen them, but you may not have noticed what he was doing. First, he lands on the edge of your plate, crawls around for a second or two, then takes off without eating a thing. It's like he's just testing you, getting a feel for your reactions, scouting the lay of the land, plotting his strategy. That little critter already knows that, to distract you, all he has to do is land on your potato salad or one of your other sides. It's always the sides, you see, for while you're busily unfolding a napkin to cover your plate, he can then pounce on what he really came for in the first place . . . your precious barbeque. (Admit it, once a fly lands on your meat, you may as well throw the whole plate away.) But pretending not to care about your meat is all a part of his game.

"You're not fooling me," you mumble. "I know what you came after."

If flies could think, he'd probably be saying, "Soon, my dear, soon. In due time I'll get my prey, but first, I must beat you at *your* game of Dodge-the-Hand."

You swat at him several times, but like a football ninja, he makes a quick dash left, then right, and lands right back in the *same* spot on your plate. You shoo him off, and he circles around your head a few times then darts right back, this time, though, a millimeter closer to your baked beans. He thinks you don't know what he's doing, but you do.

"Hey Ray-Ray," you yell to your cousin Bennie's boy. "Bring me a fly swatter from the kitchen."

After what seems like an eternity, Ray-Ray finally emerges through the back door and hands you the swatter. Your weapon of war now in hand, you ready yourself, stealthily waiting, and waiting, and waiting. Now, all of a sudden, the little bugger is nowhere to be found. "Where did you disappear to, you little creeper? I can't see you but I can feel those five, grubby little eyes staring at me."

Suddenly aware that you've been sitting there while your food gets cold, you lay the swatter down, and no sooner than you do, he plays his hand. The swatter has barely touched the ground when, out of nowhere, he's back. That's when you finally realize that if you're going to get any food in your stomach at all, you may as well resign yourself to playing *his* game of eat-and-fan.

As bothersome as flies are, some people think mosquitos are worse. Why? First of all, flies just want to eat your *food*, but mosquitos want to eat *you*. Second, they're so tiny. And third, they're so sneaky and vindictive.

If you don't believe me, just try relaxing on your patio, or taking a nap in your hammock. Not even a screened-in gazebo can keep out that *one, determined* mosquito. Why won't he stay with the throng of mosquitos crowding around the stale water in the bird bath? Why won't he stick himself to the glue strip hanging over your door or fly into the blue light of the bug zapper like he's supposed to? Instead, he keeps flying around your head like a Kamakazi pilot?

You fan him away, and for *three* seconds you have peace, but before you can take a breath, he's back. You slap at him and he flies off, but you can still feel him somewhere plotting, scheming, watching and waiting patiently. And just when you're losing the battle with the Sandman, and your eyelids are just about to meet as you drift off into lala land, he pounces! Nnnnnnnnn. Nnnnnnnnn. That's him buzzing in your ear. Nnnnnnnnn. Nnnnnnnnn.

You finally drag yourself to the shed and pull out the mosquito coil, cursing yourself for not having lit it in the first place. When you get back, there's no sign of him, but darn it, now the moment's passed and since you can't get back the full pleasure of that first "drifting off," you may as well get up and do something.

You may be thinking, "Why didn't I just put on some insect repellant in the first place?" But when you think about today's insect repellents, it's not worth the bother to put up with the stickiness, the smell and the constant reapplying. Besides, it's not generally applied in certain spots anyway, like your hair and face, the very places mosquitos like to attack.

Bug sprays may be another option, but today's bug sprays just aren't what they used to be. With the old-timey stuff, all you had to do was "ssst-ssst" for two seconds and bugs dropped from the air like lead pellets. With today's sprays, it takes bugs days to die, if at all. You can fill a room with a big cloud of it, and bugs fly leisurely through the cloud like they're on a Sunday afternoon drive in the country. They float through the mist, sniff it, and say, "Oooo, thanks for the eau de cologne," then continue their relaxing cruise around your house. You, on the other hand, sit in the other room, hacking up a lung while you wait for the fumes to clear, only to realize that the only one you're killing is yourself.

Flies and mosquitos. Mosquitos and flies.

There's one more culprit to which this saga belies. (You're welcome. You get that little rhyme for free.)

The annoying *ones* are not limited to insects. Do you remember sitting in school, working feverishly on an assignment that the teacher gave the whole class? The room was so quiet you could hear a pin drop. Then, out of nowhere, comes this weird noise. The teacher looks up, and all the students look at each other, but nobody says a word. As soon as everyone settles back into their work, there it is again – that weird noise – only this time, it's followed by a wad of paper that whizzes past your head and hits the student in front of you. One-by-one students begin to giggle because by now, everyone knows exactly who caused the disruption: none other than that *one* class clown who abominates peace and quiet. Before you know it, the whole class is in an uproar.

Flies, mosquitos, and class clowns. Yes, it's easy to point a finger at that *one bad* thing because it stands out like a sore thumb. As the saying goes, "It only takes one bad apple to spoil the whole bunch." But have you ever asked yourself why? (Here's where you need to hold on to your seats. I'm about to make a hard shift.)

"Why?" is the question that my friend, Edith, asked me one day when we were discussing our Sunday School lesson. "Why do we let that one *bad* apple spoil the whole bunch? Why can't the one *good* apple influence the whole crop?"

Edith had a point. After all, *good* – by our treasured beliefs – is more powerful than bad. In the same way that victory conquers defeat, happiness combats sadness, and love triumphs over hate, *goodness* outweighs wickedness. It only takes *one good* person to show up, stand up, or speak up, to make a difference.

Recall all the times that it took only *one good* deed to change history.

In 1955, it took only *one* woman to become the symbol for racial equality and justice by refusing to give up her seat on a bus. By comparison, it took only *one* man to lead a nation to non-violent, social change. Not only that, but in my city of Durham, North Carolina, it took the courage of *one* woman, Dr.

Lucinda McCauley Harris, to start
Durham Business College, a private
institution that prepared hundreds of
young people for the world of
business. In the same city, it took the
courage and dream of *one* man, Dr.
James E. Shepherd, to establish a college that is now
North Carolina Central University.

You may be saying that there are no more Rosa
Parkses or Martin Luther Kings or Lucinda Harrises or
James Shepherds, but there are some Jamaals and
Dorothys, and DaQuans, and Tanishas, and Nats, and a
myriad of others who can be that one. The point is,
anyone can be that *one* for positive change. Why not
you?

The Monster Inside

Portia was well into the fourth day of a special seven-day "eat healthy" diet. For lunch she had eaten green beans, baked chicken, two tablespoons of mashed potatoes, and topped it all off with two glasses of water.

Well on her way to losing her first ten pounds, she knew better than to venture too closely to the ever-present vending machine room at work. She called it the "cave of no return." In there dwelt those dreaded dragons of delight – tantalizing Twinkies®, seductive Snickers®, overpowering potato chips, and all sorts of other tenacious temptors.

All week long she had avoided the area by using the water fountain on the other end of the hall. She knew that if she even strayed into the *light* of the cave, she might be snared by the fingers of those delectable delicacies.

Today, however, the inevitable happened. A colleague, Jim Shelton, had asked her to come to his office and debug a new computer program, and his office was two doors down from the "dragon's lair." There was no way she could avoid passing it, so she devised a plan. If she walked fast, and rushed past the vending area without even glancing in its direction, maybe she could avert its alure. Her plan worked . . . *almost*. As luck would have it, just as she was within three feet of Jim's door, she heard those all-too-familiar sounds coming from inside the cave. "Ping! Clink! Clack! Thud!" Judging from the sound of it, someone had just bought a slice of Granny's Brand, chocolate layer cake with double-fudge icing. In an instant, the thought of it spun her around in her tracks, and she found herself headed toward the cavern. "No! I won't do it!" she said aloud, and turned away quickly, but before she could take one step, there it was again. That sound. This time, "Pang! Thunk! Clunk!" She knew that tone, too. A triple decker Moon Pie® fell to the shute below. She had to do something quick before it was too late, so she rushed to the water fountain and took several long gulps. As the cool liquid trickled down her throat, she turned her thoughts to what she planned to do after work: the round of tennis she planned to play; the warm sauna; a good book.

Portia took in a deep breath. "Ahhhh," she said, as she exhaled "That was close." She took another swallow of water and proceeded on to Jim's office.

As it turns out, the computer program took only a few minutes to debug and when Portia finished, she dashed to the water fountain for another quick drink, then turned to go down the hall to her office. That was when she heard them, the sweet Sirens song coming from the vending area. "I've got to be dreaming," she said. "Either that, or hallucinating."

Reassuring herself that it was all in her mind, she shook her head to clear the cobwebs, but the "songs" caused her thoughts to fade into surealistic swirls in her head. In an instant, she lost consciousness to everything around her as she fell victim to the sweet, intoxicating reverberations that seemed to lift her off the floor and draw her closer to the mouth of the cave. She was hopelessly intwined in its mystical web of estatic temptation. Like fingers of an invisible hand, the resonance drew her closer, closer, and she floated helplessly toward the second vending machine from the left. There, on the third row from the bottom – slot 2E – sat the very last triple decker Moon Pie®! Mesmerized by the thought of gooey marshmellow, sandwiched between two delicious graham crusts, and coated with smooth, rich chocolate, it seemed to shake and quiver in the wire rings that was its home . . . for now.

Portia could have sworn she heard it speak to her in a ghost-like refrain that bounced off her eardrums, "Come get me-e-e. I've been waiting for you-u-u." She put my hand over her ears, but the words still echoed in her brain, "I'm here-re-re. I'm wai-ai-ting. Come get me-e-e."

Suddenly, she found myself catapulted toward the machine, failing in all her feeble attempts to resist. As if guided by unseen forces, her hand feverishly groped inside her pocket and came out with two quarters, three nickels, and a dime. She poked them into the machine and pressed the buttons, 2, followed by E, and waited in anticipation.

To Portia's horror, nothing happened. First, disbelief, then panic, ripped through her. Had she pressed the wrong buttons? Was the machine out of order?

Suddenly she became aware of the flashing yellow light over the coin slot. "Purchase is 85 cents," it read. "Eighty-five cents?!" she uttered. "When did they changed the price?!" She shrank in terror. Those were her last coins!

Her body flushed with heat. Her scalp itched. Perspiration beaded on her forehead. What should she do?

Suddenly, the sound of footsteps coming toward the vending area shook her from her reverie. Horrifying thoughts ran through her mind. "What if someone usurps my place at the vending machine and steals my cake!?" To avert that threat, she backed against the machine and spread my arms loosely across the front of the glass. Presently, Jim Shelton's face emerged around the corner.

"Quick!" she said, pulling on the sleeve of his cardigan. "I need a dime, fast!"

"But I thought you were on a diet," Jim injected, curiously, quickly sizing up the situation. Then he added, "Na-aw-aw. I see what's going on here and I'm not going to be the one who causes your defeat."

Funny, and as unlikely as it was, at that moment Portia understood how desparate people could commit unexpected acts against others. It's also when she understood why people struggling with all kinds of addictions often fall off the wagon. She understood how it starts with a mental picture of yourself taking that first drink, or hit, or bite of food. Then it moves to imagining the pleasure of it. And if you give in, then the cravings start. They get bigger and stronger. Then somehow you find yourself surrounded by the very thing you're trying to avoid. Everywhere you turn someone is mixing a drink, or opening a candy wrapper, or cooking your favorite food. You pull away. You run. You try everything to get away but it just seems that the "it" is out to get you.

Despite the end result of the scenerio that played in Portia's mind, she still pictured herself taking that first bite of Moon Pie®. She could taste the marshmallowy goodness, mingled with its special ingredient that gave it that distinctive taste. She savored the image in her mind, while feeding on the sensations pulsating through her body, the orgasmic ripples that sent waves of passion through her tastebuds. The thought of the delectable morsel sliding sensuously past her palate was more than she could handle. She had been taken over by an entity, a shadow of her rational self, and it reduced her to a weak heap of flesh, begging for a sucrose fix that she knew she didn't need.

"But Jim, it'll only be this one time," she pleaded.

"Yeah, that's what you say now. That's what they *all* say. But these things have a way of snowballing. Look. You've already lost a lot. Why I can tell the difference myself. Please don't give in. If you just turn away now the craving will pass."

Images of a new, thinner self flashed through Portia's mind (and the key word here is "flashed"). Jim made sense, and she hated it when people made sense while you're in the throes of cravings. It just makes you have to beg that much harder. So she pulled out her imaginary knee pads and gave it another try.

"Jim, please. I promise. Once I eat this one cake I'll continue right on with my diet."

She paused, waited for that to sink in, then hit him him below the belt with the old "experts say" line.

"Besides, experts say that if you have a craving that absolutely won't go away, you should eat just a little bit of the food that you crave so you won't binge on something else."

He mellowed. She saw the little lines of sympathy form in the corner of his eyes. "Got him!" Her heart leaped for joy, but she wasn't fully satisfied. She needed to hit him while he was down with one more dose, just for good measure.

"And Jim. You know I've been so goo-o-d. I haven't cheated. Not one, single, time. Surely, just this once won't hurt. You know I always keep my word. And I promise not to let this stop me. As soon as I have this one snack, I promise I'll continue on with my diet as if nothing every happened." For good measure, she sealed her promises with her best, most sincere, pitiful face.

Her excitement built as she saw Jim reach into his pants pocket and pull out two nickels. Oh those precious shiney coins! Her eyes clung to them like a soul clinging to life itself.

"Thanks Jim," she said as she grabbed them from his hand and spun around to the machine. Her hands shook as she shoved the coins into the slot. "Plunk, plunk, clank." Oh the sweet sounds of coins turning the tumblers in the automatic coin counter!

"Whirrrrr," the motor whined and cranked. The little spirals turned. One-quarter turn. Two-quarter turns. Three-quarter turns. Then silence. An empty, horrifying hollowness cut through Portia's gut. There, hanging in limbo, was her precious cake, pinched between the spirals and the bottom edge of the shelf.

"Awwgggggggggggggggggggggh!! Oh noooooo!!" She let out a loud yell that brought people streaming from their offices. Jim took charge and explained the situation quickly. One-by-one all the others looked at Portia, shook their heads, and walked away, leaving her and there Jim alone. No one offered sympathy. And darn it, no one offered to loan her any more money.

"Look at it this way," Jim finally spoke up. "After all you went through to get that cake and you *still* didn't succeed, it must not have been meant for you to have it." With that, he, too, turned and walked away, leaving Portia staring blankly at the machine in silent disbelief, licking the tears that trickled down her face and into the corners of her mouth.

PART II: PERSONAL GROWTH

Personal growth is generally defined as an ongoing process of self-discovery and improvement. While personal growth may be difficult, on the flip side, it can be very rewarding and enlightening. Although the process of growing is not always easy, the things that we learn through personal growth can bring knowledge, power, and everlasting freedom.

Some Things I've Learned Over the Years

As I approach eighty, I've learned that there are a
lot of things I learned when I didn't know I was
learning them, but years after I learned them, I learned
that I was happy I had learned them. Twisted? I meant
for it to be. It's an attention grabber folks. All I'm
saying is this: When we are older and more mature, we
look back over our lives and realize that all the insights
we acquired – through our parents, in school, our
experiences and life lessons – were valuable, even
though we didn't recognize, or appreciate them at the
time. I don't know what your journey through life has
been like, but maybe you can relate to some of the
things *I've* learned.

1. I've learned that I don't need all the stuff I once
    thought I couldn't *possibly* live without. I used to
    think that owning the biggest house on the block, or
    the biggest, flashiest, most expensive car was so
    great. I once owned all of that stuff and more. Big
    whoop. I'm over it.
2. I've learned that it's easier to let go of things that I
    don't use anymore. I don't need "things" in my
    house just because they look pretty or fit into a
    certain place. For example, why do I need a china
    closet full of dishes that I never use? Why do I need
    furniture that no one ever sits on, in a room where
    no one ever goes?
3. I've learned to let go of my worry and anxiety
    about people's opinions of me.

4. I've learned to hold on to things that truly matter, such as faith, family, and true friends.

5. I've learned that I don't need to check every word before I speak just because I'm afraid of offending someone (although I don't deliberately offend).

6. I've learned not to rush so much. As the saying goes, "Haste makes waste." When you rush, you tend to forget things, lose things, misplace things, or break something.

7. I've learned that I don't fear death. Dying, on the other hand, is a whole different story, and yes, they are two different things. Death is "poof!" and you're gone. One nanosecond you're here and the next nanosecond you're on the other side. Dying, alternatively, is a slow process that actually begins the moment we are born. Dying takes years, and you do so by degrees, in slow increments of time. It encompasses aging, ailments, ups and downs, highs and lows. And God forbid that you end up incapacitated, or in a shoddy nursing home, or both! All this may sound morbid and pessimistic, but it's realistic. What we call "living" is actually dying. Dying ain't for sissies.

8. I've learned to find awe and wonder in God's creations: a baby's tiny hands, the blue of the sky, the bark on trees, flowers, grass, raindrops, streams, rivers, oceans, stars, and so many other things too numerous to name.

9. I've learned that God is the creator of time, and with God, time is infinite. It has no end. It's fluid. Mankind is the one who takes God's time and tries to manipulate it by putting it into smaller segments

of seconds, minutes, hours, days, etc., etc. I believe that time, as we know it, does not carry the same significance with God. We are the ones who add significance to time by trying to fit God's time into our predetermined segments. That's why we get so frustrated when things don't work out when we think they ought to work out, that is, on our time schedule. I think we're better off relaxing and allowing God to take care of things in God's own "time."

10. I've learned that a smile dispels fear, anger, and sometimes hate in others.

11. I've learned not to retaliate in anger or seek revenge.

12. I've learned that if you remain calm in chaotic situations, you can think clearer.

13. I've learned not to question people who have big egos unless you think your ego is bigger, or you are confident enough to withstand their pushback. People with big egos get offended easily, likely because they're already thinking, "I know what I'm talking about. How dare you question me!" Challenging them only causes chaos.

14. I've learned to "choose my battles." Sometimes it's better to stand down than to get frustrated trying to prove your point, or enlighten and convince another.

15. I've learned that the greatest teacher is time, stirred into a mixture of maturity, life experiences, circumstances, and the Spirit of God.

16. I've learned that if you want to be heard, speak softer than others. Speaking softly makes loud

people listen because, in order to hear you, they have to quiet down.

17. I've learned that if you don't yell back at someone who's out of control, they will soon calm down. (It's hard for one to argue alone.) After years of trying to master this technique – and thinking that it was some new phenomenon that I had conquered – I discovered that the Bible already told us so. (Proverbs 15:1 – "A soft answer turns away wrath, but harsh words stir up anger.")

18. I've learned that you can find anything you need in the Bible. I can't think of any thought, any question, any scenario that the Bible cannot answer in some way.

19. I've learned that when young people get impatient with you because you're old and move too slowly for them, you should pray that they have a long life and a reflective memory.

20. I've learned that I don't really have any enemies. If I don't make you my enemy, then you're not my enemy, but if you view me as your enemy, then it's a contrivement of your own mind. The *Cambridge Dictionary* defines an enemy as "a person who hates or opposes another person and tries to harm them or stop them from doing something." So if *I* don't hate or oppose *you*, then *you* are not my enemy. And if *you* don't hate or oppose *me*, then *I'm* not *your* enemy. I wonder what would happen if we stopped automatically hating others because of some preconceived or predetermined notion about them? What if – instead of thinking the worst about someone – we all simply showed common

courtesy to each other? What if that common courtesy started with a simple "Good morning," or "Hello," without the fear that your greeting would be ignored? My Uncle Wallace once said, "Speaking (greeting someone) doesn't cost anything." Even if the person doesn't reciprocate, maybe by your kind gesture they'd pass it on to the next person. After all, it only takes one person to make a difference.

21. I've learned that there are ways to say "no" and still get the same results without sounding so offensive. Flatly saying "no" to a someone could create negativity towards you (depending on their maturity level). The scenario: Someone asks to borrow money. You could say "no" in this way: "Oh, I'm sorry, but I have a policy of not lending money." And you could add, "I've found that it puts a strain on relationships and I value our friendship too much." Of course, if it's a trusted friend who you know would never ask if they didn't truly need it, that's a different story.

22. I've learned that you should "count up the costs" before you start doing favors for people. An old friend once told me, "Start out the way you can hold out." In other words, if you are not prepared to continue rendering favors for the same person (or different favors for different friends) then you should not start doing favors in the first place (or at least set *very clear* limits from the beginning). Everyone needs help at some point in their life but some people make a habit of asking for help and

they will always call on you before they even try to figure it out on their own.

23. I've learned that saying, "I apologize" carries the same weight as "I'm sorry" without *you* having to wrestle with your conscience about whether you're truly sorry. "I apologize," says that you are willing to end the conflict and help bring about peace.

24. I've learned that having values is very, very important. My cousin Tyrone used to repeat a quote that is commonly attributed to Alexander Hamilton and used by others, "If you don't stand for something you'll fall for anything." I think of it this way: There ought to be something (or a few things) in your life that you absolutely refuse to do, some line you will not cross, or some value you will not compromise. A person who does not take *any* type of moral stand will do *anything* for *any* reason.

25. I've learned that at some point in our lives we are forced to look at ourselves in the mirror, examine each pane of Johari's window, and ask ourselves, "Who are you? Really, who are you, the *real* you?"

26. I've learned that what my grandma told me seems to be true about people who lie. "If a person will lie, they'll cheat, and if they'll cheat, then they'll steal, and if they'll steal, they'll kill."

27. I've learned that the power of the mind can change your life. If we stay focused on good, positive, righteous, and virtuous things, it pushes out the negative.

28. I've learned that if you keep saying "live agent" to the automated operator, you can usually bypass "her" and get to a real person.

29. I've learned that what my dad told me is true: You can't borrow your way out of debt. Every bill you make decreases your earnings, thus increasing the need to borrow more to stay afloat. He said that the best way to get ahead is to live within your income. That means denying yourself some of the things that you truly don't need, putting money in a savings account, forgetting about it and leaving it alone.

30. I've learned not to automatically assume that my answer is the only *right* answer. Actually, it's not even the *only* answer, let alone always the *right* one.

31. I've learned, above all, that we only learn what we are taught by our parents, teachers, friends, and associates, and that God opens up our understanding through epiphanies and revelations.

32. I've learned that just because you know something doesn't mean that others are wrong or ignorant. It doesn't hurt me to relinquish my rigid hold on *my* idea and listen to others. So I close this section with a true story that follows along these lines.

In 1981, my then-pastor, his wife and three or four others from the church stopped at a little fruit stand in Haw River, NC. While the others were off doing their shopping, the pastor's wife and I found ourselves at the same bin, picking out oranges.

Now my favorite, all-time orange was a juicy navel orange (not so much now, since "shrinkflation"), so when I saw her pick up an ordinary orange, I immediately took it upon myself to "school" her on the succulent navel orange, assuming, as I usually did/do, that she was just uneducated as to some of the finer qualities of life. I thought that if she ever ate one, she'd never go back to the dull, ordinary, everyday oranges.

I might mention here that at *that* time in my life, when I "knew" something, I was like a kid with a new, shiney, red ball, and *my* ball was the only one in the world. I'd be so self-absorbed with *my* "ball" (i.e., my always-right knowledge) that I never considered that manufacturers made thousands of other shiney, red balls, and I wasn't the owner of the only red ball in creation. So being locked into the belief that I had the more sophisticated taste, I felt it my duty to school the pastor's wife and help refine her tastebuds.

"Oh, you ought to try these," I said excitedly.

"No, I like these better," she replied, softly.

"But if you just try one, I bet you'll find that it's far better than those," I protested.

"No." She insisted. "These are the ones I like," she repeated, again very calmly, very softly.

In my defense, I'd like to say that my forwardness was *not* deliberate. It stemmed from my ignorance and misunderstanding of social cues. So, undeterred, I tried again, thinking that she just didn't know what she was missing. (Why is it that some people think they know what's best for you, better than you do?)

"But just *taste* one," I said, pushing it in her face. "I think you'll love it. Here. Let me buy it for you, so you can try it."

That's when she looked me dead in the eyes, her piercing glaze stopping me in my tracks. With that same calm voice, this time very emphatic and sure, she said, "Sister Evelyn. *These* are the oranges I like. *These* are the oranges I prefer."

Her directness caused the light bulb to come on in my head. It's funny how when you finally "get it," there is no anger, no frustration, no fighting back. Only acquiescence and understanding.

I wish I could say that from that time on, I never pushed myself and my ways on anyone else, but that's not the case. Bullheadness doesn't die easily. Still, that encounter taught me a valuable lesson that I shall never forget, and one that I reiterate from earlier: Just because *I* know something doesn't mean that it's the only answer or even the only *right* answer. Other people know things, too, and even if they don't, sometimes they we need to leave them alone to learn on their own, over time, in their due season.

The Oak and the Reed and Me

One of Aesop's fables tells the story of a mighty oak tree, growing next to a stream. Growing beside the oak along the same stream was a lowly reed.

The oak tree stood proud and boastful. "Just look at how tall I am and how hard my trunk and branches are!" he said, as he mocked the reed. "You, on the other hand, are so small and puny, so tiny and weak. You can't even hold up the weight of a bird."

In all of this, the reed refused to argue back. Yes, it was true, he bent at the slightest breeze, and he couldn't bear any weight, but he was happy just being a reed, so he remained cheerful and humble.

Then one day a violent thunderstorm came. The rain pummelled the reed and the wind blew so hard that it bent low to the ground under the weight of the torrent.

When the storm was over, there lay the big oak tree, broken, with its roots turned upward. With all of its might and strength, the oak had not survived. Yet, the reed sprang right back up, ready for another day in the sun.

Some say that Aesop's story is a contrast between pride and humility. Others point to the reed and say that it provides advice on how to survive in turbulent times. Still others say that the parable points out that it's wiser to be flexible sometimes than stubbornly resisting and refusing to change. I like the one on LizStoryPlanet that reads, "It is better to bend than break. It is better to be flexible than stubborn." She also adds that pride comes before a fall.

If I may, (of course I may), I'd like to expound on those thoughts because I can identify with the oak.

In my early adult life, I was proud, strong-willed, inflexible. I was so stoic that I refused to bend for anyone or any situation. I didn't show emotion of *any* kind, especially crying. I absolutely *refused* to cry . . . not for *any* reason. Crying, you see, was a sign of weakness, and in my eyes I certainly wasn't weak.

I was too blind to see people staring at me or whispering behind my back. I was too busy fighting to maintain control of my world, the one that existed only in my own mind. To me, self-preservation was key to my survival and to let anyone inside my world (or for me to "go" out into theirs) was too frightening. It meant vulnerability, weakness, loss of self. And so, I had to maintain *my* world at all costs.

That all changed in 1979 when my world came crashing in on me. I was thirty-two years old at the time and a freshman in college on a scholarship from the university where I worked. One day, while sitting in my English class, I slipped into subconsciousness. I don't know how long I was "out," but when I came back, I found myself staring at one line in the palm of my left hand. It was the most terrified moment that I'd ever had in my entire life.

If you think I rushed to the nearest emergency room, you'd be wrong. Stoicism and self-control dictate that *no* situation is greater than the person who experiences it. In other words, I viewed myself as being invincable, greater than any problem that tried to change or overtake me. So, dazed and confused, I continued my classes, yet remained on high alert the rest of the day.

Oddly, the need for a medical doctor never crossed my mind either, but later, the need for mental health help did. Still, I didn't seek help right away, which is very hard to explain. I don't think you'd understand how frightening therapy is to someone so rigid and under control. Not to mention the fact that, traditionally, Black people, *especially* strong, Black *women*, just didn't go into therapy. For me to go into therapy would tear down a centuries-old persona of the indestructible Black woman and reinforce the notion that if you go into therapy, you are weak, broken, crazy. Being the one to accept that kind of help was a line I wasn't willing (or was too afraid) to cross. Still, I knew I needed help and to get that help, I had a decision to make. I could stay stuck in a false prison of ignorance, or face the reality that I was an educated, enlightened Black woman who should know better. I could allow fear to keep me bound, or I could break those cultural taboos and get the help I knew I needed. I chose the latter.

At first, therapy was equally as terrifying as my blackout. The thought of ending up completely losing my mind paralyzed me. Still, I knew I needed to brave the unknown and conquer those grotesque, monsterous ogres – fear and self-control – that had kept me bound for most of my life.

I confess that therapy did start out rough at first. For the first time ever, I had to face who I was, who I *truly* was. I had to see myself from the outside looking in, rather than the *inside*, looking deeper *inside*. I had to face all my flaws, my idiosyncrasies, my fears, and most terrifying for me, my need for self-control. (This, I learned, was partially the source of my intense anger and anxiety.) I also learned that part of my competitiveness stemmed from my need to prove myself – to me – and to others. This need, in turn, stemmed from my inferiority complex.

It took months for me to gain a new sense of *self* and appreciate the fact that I was worthy to *live*. (Yes, I mean *live*, because many years earlier, shortly after graduating high school, I had attempted suicide by walking in front of a car. Only the quick actions of my friends saved me.) I also came to accept the fact that therapy was a valuable tool to maintain balance in my life and that I need not be ashamed to ask for help. I learned that asking for help was actually a sign of bravery and strength, not cowardice and weakness. As it turned out, therapy ended up being the *second* best thing that ever happened to me (the first being salvation).

As I look back, I'm so grateful for that blackout. If it had not been for that one, lost space of time, I may never have known me, the *real* me, and the *real* me, I discovered, is ten thousand times better than the chimerical me. The real *me* began to feel emotions, empathy, sympathy, joy. The *real* me began to laugh. The *real* me started to enjoy life. The *real* me is more authentic. All this, and more, happened because I took a chance on therapy, for it was in therapy that, for the first time as an adult, I cried.

Jesus: A Matter of Faith

It perplexes me how people will do *anything* to keep from believing in Jesus. They spend more time and energy trying to discredit, deny, and outright avoid even the mention of His name, than they do simply accepting Him. They don't realize that by raging an all-out war *against* Jesus, they are unwittingly fulfilling the prophecies of the very Book that declared His authority and priesthood, and at the same time they expose their heresy.

For the sake of argument, let's lay aside atheists and agnostics (groups that do not believe in the existence of God and those who question the existence of God). That is not at issue here. Besides, if their minds are made up, there is nothing that anyone can say to convince them otherwise. It would take One greater than us – the Spirit of the very God they deny – to convince them. Let me digress here to tell you a little story.

Over fifteen years ago, I saw a newscast about a little boy who had gone missing. Everyone searched frantically to find the little boy with no results. They were about to give up hope when suddenly a middle-aged man emerged from the woods carrying the boy to safety. The reporter who interviewed the man asked him how he managed to find the boy when no one else could. Here was his reply: "Well, I don't believe in God and all that, but I prayed, 'God, if there's a God out there, let me find that boy.' And then I found him."

I often wondered if finding that boy so quickly after praying changed the man's belief in God. I hope it did, and I hope others will find something that changes their minds about the existence of God, and not only a belief in God's existence, but also a connection with Jesus the Christ.

So why do so many people go to such great lengths to "ward off" Jesus? Could it be fear of the truth, that what they've heard all their lives about the existence of Jesus is a reality? Could it be fear of change, that somehow they think that if they believe in Jesus fully, they would change into some type of Bible-thumping fanatic? Could it be that they love their actions, behaviors and lifestyle too much to explore anything different? Or, could it be that they simply do not want to take a cold, hard look at themselves the way they think God looks at them? Maybe they are afraid of what they would find if they looked deeply within themselves. Maybe connecting with the God-conscientiousness is the very fear that paralyzes them. It's like trying to convince a person who's dead set against being introspective that introspection is the very thing that will break any yoke of bondage. I wonder, do people fight introspection because it makes them feel vulnerable? Are they afraid to expose their real selves and see who they really are? After all, as Michael Jackson implied, who wants to face "the man in the mirror"? Finding out the truth about one's self is, or can be, a crumbling fear. Yet that crumbling fear – hitting the bottom of the barrel, if you will – is the very thing that brings us to the light. From the bottom of the barrel, the only other place to go is up, and up is liberating. Up brings hope. Up is enlightening and encouraging. Up is exciting and new. Up brings a world of new possibilities. So who wouldn't want to be up?

If you're looking for a simple answer to the question of who wouldn't want to be up, there is no simple answer, but I can offer my opinion, an opinion from someone who has "been there." For my answer, I offer this scenario:

Imagine that you're fairly new in town, and so far you've enjoyed everything you've seen. On this particular night, you decide to go for a walk just to get out of the house. Once on the sidewalk, you call a friend to chat with while you walk. You get so immersed in conversation that twenty minutes later, you realize you've walked into an unfamiliar section of town. The sidewalks are devoid of people; the streetlights are old and faded; and the only illumination is coming from the neon lights inside the businesses lining the sidewalks. If only you had paid more attention to where you were going along your walk! Panic begins to set in and every sound is magnified. You call an Uber, but it'll be a while. A half block away you see a bright light streaming from a store around the corner. The most logical thing to do is to head for the light, but you don't know what you'll find when you get there. Will it really be a business, or just a streetlight that's shining brighter than the rest? And if it's a business, will it be open? And if it is open, what type of people might be inside? So many uncertainties, but one thing you know for sure is that you are not safe staying where you are. If only you had some way of knowing – ahead of time – what you will find around that corner. But of course there is no crystal ball, no

*forecaster, no seer, just you with the darkness closing
in, and that one, bright light up ahead. You sense that
there is safety in that light, but you are too afraid to
trust that what you feel is true. Yet the only way you'll
find out is to take that step toward the light.*

This scenario probably details what many people
think about Jesus. They know that He is their refuge
from troubles but are afraid to trust Him because they
fear what they might find. Staying in one's comfort
zone is far less frightening than going into the
unknown, even if that unknown appears to be a saving
grace. If only there was some way to see on "the other
side" of trusting Jesus before they actually trust Him.
Of course, that's not possible. It's like opening a
Cracker Jack® box. You can't see the prize inside until
you search through the popcorn and tear open the
wrapper that contains the toy. And just like the person
in the story, you can't see what's around the corner
until you actually turn the corner. To do that you must
trust that what's on the other side is better than what
you have now. You can't possibly know the freedom,
the peace, the love, the joy of knowing Jesus until you
actually walk around that corner into the Light. And
this I *do* know from self-experience: Walking around
that corner is worth it.

To Be Apart or To Be A Part
That Is the Question (and the message within)

Okay, I get it. I get it people, those of you who like privacy. I get it, those of you who find better company in themselves than with others. I get it, those of you who would check the box marked "does not play well with others" on a psychological test. I get it, the loners, the pensive, those who want solitude. I get it because *I* fall into the same category.

Yes, we do love our privacy, don't we, and we can see ourselves living off the grid. Well, I can *see* it but I wouldn't, actually *do* it *personally*, because I'm too afraid of snakes and bugs, and worms, and such. Still, I admire and envy those who do live off the grid.

Living off the grid has many advantages. For example, you can live healthier. You can grow your own food (or hunt for it) if you so choose. You don't encounter pollutants from vehicles and industry, like you would in crowded cities. You can also avoid germs from crowds and sick animals. Also, you don't have to contend with city noises and overcrowding. That alone would probably drop your stress level as you unwind in nature. Oh yes, and don't forget the *big* advantage of no utility bills!

Another advantage of living off the grid for me is having complete control over your life. You can have your own system of survival (and, for the most part, your own system of government too).

Admittedly, I never lived completely off the grid, but during my early years, my family lived *semi*-off the grid. My father owned a ten-acre farm about three miles from the nearest town (and the town itself was small and rural). Life was grand. We had chickens, hogs, cows, and lots of land (at least it seemed like a lot of land to me, because when you're a five-year-old little girl, ten acres looks like a hundred). Our well supplied all the water we needed, crops supplied food, and the whole farm was our playground.

Then my family moved into town to be closer to my dad's grocery store he had built some years earlier. We lived on the west side of town on a dirt road in a small congested neighborhood called "The Bottom." For the first time in my life, I was bombarded with traffic, houses all around me, and people who dropped in unannounced. I felt intruded upon. And to make matters worse, our house was on a small hill, on a corner lot. This always made me feel like a caged animal at the zoo or a fish trapped in a fishbowl.

When I reached adulthood, I moved out of that neighborhood and bought a house on a half-acre of land, surrounded by woods. Ahhhh. Heaven! No one visited. No one meddled. No one kept me from doing what *I* wanted to do, when *I* wanted to do it, and most importantly, no more fishbowls. Life was grand. I was as "snug as a bug in a rug."

The funny thing about life is that it has a way of progressing and changing around you, and when that happens, you have to decide whether you want to change along with it or stay stuck in the past. In due time, that question came knocking on my door in the form of career moves. As my career choices changed, so did my attitude toward being isolated. Oh, I liked my privacy (and still do to this day) but the

professional pathway that I took brought me to
Durham, where I connected with people of different
cultures and backgrounds, and viewpoints. Being in a
different environment not only helped me mature, but it
also caused me to think about my place in an ever-
changing world. Did I want to continue being isolated,
or did I want to mingle, absorb and learn what others
had to offer? I chose the latter – to be a *part* – and it
turned out to be the best choice for me.

Learning to live amongst people brought me out of
my shell. No longer was my world view limited to what
my parents and grandparents knew, or what I'd learned
on the farm, or in my small neighborhood, or read
about in books. Being around "city people" taught me
sophisticated social graces and how to behave in
different settings. I learned when to speak and when to
keep silent (and what to say, or *not* say, if is did speak).
I learned *how* to trust and *who* to trust (or not trust). I
also learned to read facial expressions and pick up on
innuendos and outright lies. My cognitive and
socialization skills increased, as did my enjoyment of
life. I was invited to parties and sophisticated social
gatherings. I went on trips and saw so much more of
this country than ever before. Because of my job and
connection to people, I even met judges and senators
and famous historians. I also got the chance to visit
other countries, something that being *apart* only
manifested in my dreams.

In the end, I'm not advocating that "grid dwellers"
should give up their grid life, or that city dwellers
should go off the grid. Both have their advantages and
disadvantages, and no matter the choice, you can

always change your mind. For me, these days, I have a little of both. I live on the outskirts of Durham in an area that is a little rural but not without modern conveniences. I have restaurants and grocery stores within walking distance, a river and park across the street, a clinic a block away, and a hospital within two miles. Yes, I miss the open air and freedom of my farm, but for me, now that I'm almost eighty, being a *part* is a good trade-off.

Oops. For those of you who may be still scratching your heads and getting mad at me because I didn't point out the message within, here it is: Living off the grid was not the *only* point of this writing. It was also about making a decision to be a *part* of something greater than yourself – where you interact, learn and grow – or being *apart* (isolating (in mind or body)) from the greater society. There is actually no right or wrong answer, I guess, only the answer that's right for you.

A Mostly True Story

One day, I stopped to eat lunch at a little country cafe in the eastern part of Durham. After getting my food, I went to the farthest table in back to eat. (Since COVID, I avoid crowds whenever I can.)

Shortly, a neatly dressed man came in. He got his food and sat in the empty booth near the door. Sitting a few feet from him were two City workers who talked across the aisle to each other. (Why they didn't sit at the same table, I have no clue.) One worker said something to his co-worker, who replied, "This is [bleep] good." By proximity of his seat, surely the man at the door heard it, but he never reacted. Without hesitation, he removed his hat, prayed over his food, and ate it in silence. Another "bleep" word and the man at the door looked at the City worker with raised brow, but continued eating as if nothing had happened. I, on the other hand, couldn't clear my head of the worker's uninhibited use of profanity in public. In my mind, I saw myself zapping him, and for good measure, everyone else who cussed. It reminded me of stories I'd heard of Catholic nuns who popped students with a ruler when they misbehaved.

As I sat there stewing, my mind drifted (as it often does). I imagined myself having a conversation with God in prayer. In my conversation, I said, "God, I wish I could stop everyone in the world from cussin'" and God said, "Pray and don't *you* use profanity." Then I said, "While I'm at it, God, I wish I could end hatred," and God said, "Pray and don't hate anyone." Yet again I said, "God, I wish I could do something about peoples' judgmental attitudes," and God said, "Pray and don't judge." Then I said, "God, why is it that every time I ask you something, you tell me to pray and don't do this or that?" And God said, "Pray as if it all depends on me, but work as if it all depends on you. Don't expect me to everything. Change must begin within people. *You* be the change." And so I finished my lunch with "saying" another word and left, quietly, wiser than when I came.

Thank You, Young Folks

As members of the "older generation," we septuagenarians, octogenarians and beyond, tend to call anyone under the age of forty, "young folk," especially Millennials, Gen Ys and Gen Zs. We spend a lot of time disparaging them, and often lump them all into the same category. We forget that there are many "young folk" who contribute so much to society. We forget to praise them for the wonderful things they do. So here's to you young folks. Thank you for . . .

- respecting others, especially your parents, grandparents and all elders
- staying in school
- seeking a higher education
- working and keeping a job
- holding down job(s) while going to school
- staying out of trouble
- saying, "Yes ma'am, yes sir, no ma'am, no sir"
- opening/holding doors open for others
- helping old and disabled people
- being kind and courteous to everyone
- respecting your parents, especially your mother
- cleaning your room without being told and without fussing
- going to church without fussing
- playing sports
- not loitering on sidewalks, in front of businesses and on street corners
- walking with your head held high

- playing an instrument
- singing and/or dancing
- not sneaking out at night
- boys, not getting your girlfriend pregnant
- girls, not sleeping around with boys
- not lying, especially to your parents
- boys, wearing your pants on your waist
- not participating in the use, sale or dealing with drugs in any way
- praying
- not using the "b" word
- not using foul language, especially in public

And for all the *other* good, propserous things that you do, for which no one ever says "thank you," let me be the first to say that we appreciate you! Thank you young people. Keep up the good work!

In Praise Of Nerds

Nerd" is not a dirty word. It is a word used by bullies, and people who try to dominate others in order to feel better about themselves. People who call you a nerd are jealous and weak. They are succumbing to peer pressure rather than being a leader. If people call you a nerd because you study hard and stay focused, it's because they can't see that you are working toward a goal. They only see the *now* in you, but not the *later*. They don't see the future *you*, the person who you will become because of your perseverance.

"Nerds" strive to reach above and beyond. They seek professions that require specific, higher education. They choose careers that they expect to be their life-long work. If anyone calls you a nerd (or if you think that being a "nerd" is bad), take a look at just a few of the careers that nerds have:

- Brand manager
- Computer Programer or Analysts
- Chief Executive Officer (CEO)
- Chief Financial Officer (CFO)
- Chief Marketing Officer (CMO)
- Chief Operating Officer (COO)
- Chief Information Officer (CIO)
- Doctor
- Marketing Specialist
- Nurse
- Product Manager
- Public Relations Manager

- Scientist
- Search Engine Optimization Manager
- Social Media Manager

So keep studying, keep working, keep striving, keep moving upward. You *will* succeed, and when you become the head of your department, company, division or region; when you become the chief of this or that; when you are the owner of a company, don't forget to be kind to your former haters when they come to you for a job.

It's Not Nice to Fool With Mother Nature

What if Mother Nature had hands, real hands, like human hands. If she did, would she toss paper bags, cigarette butts, and the like, back at people who litter? Would she toss every can, bottle or food scrap back inside peoples' cars as they drove by?

What if Mother Nature decided to create an unavoidable, mud-filled pothole directly in front of every driver who littered? Do you think they'd finally "get it" if it happened every time tossed something?

If Mother Nature had hands, would her mighty fingers skim all the oceans, and collect the tons of plastic bottles, cans, discarded fishing nets, and other debris left behind by humans? Do you think caves would vomit up the same? Do you think Mother Nature would call upon the winds to travel to the ends of the earth and drop each piece of trash back in the yard of the person who tossed it out in the first place?

What if Mother Nature had a voice, a real voice, like a human voice? Do you imagine she'd say, "Help! [cough] I'm choking on your pollution, [cough] and if I can't breathe, you won't have oxygen?" Do you think she'd add, "And please leave some trees standing. Every vacant piece of land doesn't need to be turned into a mall or housing development."

If Mother Nature had a voice, would she let out a deafening roar every time someone shot an elephant for its tusks, or a rhinoceros for its horn? Would she scream every time a hunter killed a tiger or alligator for their skin?

Does Mother Nature have feelings? Does she feel pain every time we carve graffiti on her hills or in the bark of her trees?

Does Mother Nature have a heart? Do we break it every time we abuse her or mistreat each other?

Ahhh, but if we look around, and take in all that Mother Nature is, we find that she indeed has hands and a voice, and much more. Could that be her tears in the sap of weeping willow trees? Could the dried up riverbeds and streams be the constriction of her "blood vessels"?

Does Mother Nature get sick? Does it mean that she has contracted a virus when we start to see blighted trees that have never been affected before?

Is Mother Nature trying to tell us something with strange weather patterns? Is she speaking through record-breaking high temperatures, or severe precipitation, or drought conditions? Or maybe it's the increase in cyclones and hurricanes or melting icecaps. What about the lack of winter months and early blooming springs? Does Mother Nature still love us?

Ohh, but wait. Yes, we see that Mother Nature still loves us, despite what we do to her. She watches us, and she watches *over* us, all the time. She sees us through the eyes of the aspen tree and in the broken branches of the birch. She watches us through the eyes of squirrels, rabbits and deer, every time they stand still, pondering, contemplating.

Mother Nature's voice sings to us through every bird's song and with the buzzing of bees. She speaks to us with the rustling of leaves and the babbling of brooks.

Mother Nature hears us in the echoes of a thousand caves and hollow valleys, then sings back to us in sweet refrain.

Mother Nature's arms caress us with warm ocean breezes and bathes us with sunshine and warmth.

Yes, Mother Nature loves us, and I *know* it's love because she is patient and kind, and no matter what we do to her, she keeps on giving.

PART III: SOCIAL COMMENTARIES
(not for those easily offended)

Do you ever get tired of guarding your words? Do you keep certain thoughts and opinions hidden inside. Do you conceal the things you dare not share with anyone but your inner circle, and sometimes not even with them?

That's how I feel sometimes, and I assume others feel the same way. This section addresses some socially and politically hot topics that many people are reluctant to discuss, so as the subtitle warns, this section is not for those easily offended because it's provocative, bold, and direct. Some of the topics contain things that people might say to their closest friends, in private, and when their friends look shocked, they'd say, "C'mon. You know you were *thinking* it."

Rethinking Controversy

What is controversy? One definition of controversy is this: a disagreement, typically prolonged, public, and heated. My question: Does it have to be prolonged, public and heated to be a controversy? Can any disagreement be classified as controversial? Do we create controversy simply by disagreeing with someone? In my opinion, *anything* can be made controversial.

It's easy to recognize controversy when it comes to big, nationwide subjects like abortion, gun control, global warming, and Affirmative Action. Even smaller, local issues like not letting the class Valedictorian speak at UNC's graduation, or inviting Jerry Seinfeld to speak at Duke's graduation sparked controversy. However, when I say that anything can be controversial, I truly mean *anything*. No subject is off limits. It only takes one person to disagree with something that someone says or does to cause a controversy. Here's an example:

Until the late-1970s, you probably never thought twice about eating a steak and baked potato at a fancy restaurant. Nor did people see any harm in killing weeds with their favorite weed killer or putting food in plastic containers. But now, many deem red meat to be bad for you. Likewise, some people switched to eating baked *sweet* potatoes (not the same taste, people), and their favorite weed killer has been reformulated. Not to mention that using plastic in any form gets a few raised eyebrow these days.

I'm not opposed to anyone taking a stand against certain things and discontinuing their use. Nor am I against anyone who continues to use them (I being in the latter category). But think about this: With trillions of people in the United States, everybody can't have *everything* they want *all* the time. Sensibility calls for compromise. We shouldn't turn every little thing into a controversy just because it's something we don't like. In short, whatever the *that* is to you, won't be *that* if you don't make it *that*.

A Couple of Controversial Issues

Speaking of controversy, here are my thoughts and opinions on two of the most controversial issues in America today. Again, I remind you that these are *my* thoughts and opinions, so please don't start any splinter groups because of me.

The Abortion Issue. As unpopular as my opinion may be, I'm *against* abortion. I believe an embryo is alive. It's a baby – perhaps without appendages, eyes, intestines, etc. – but a baby nonetheless, in jelly-like form.

According to what I've found in my research, the embryotic stage exists from conception (during intercourse) to 7 or 8 weeks. After eight weeks, it's a fetus. *Now* I understand why – back in my day – it was unsafe (or, perhaps, inhuman) for a woman to have an abortion after eight weeks. Back then, doctors wouldn't even perform abortions after that stage of pregnancy. I guess they understood that it wasn't *just* a "jelly glob."

The concept of life is a no-brainer to me. Sperm cells are alive (naturally because they come from a *live* human male). In fact, sperm can live up to five days. Likewise, a woman's egg is a *living* organism (also from a *live* human female), but it lives for only twelve to twenty-four hours. That in itself is the first miracle of conception. To think that in that little span of time, a woman can conceive.

From here, it's simply a matter of applying the If-And-Then-Therefore logical principle that you learned in college: IF a sperm is already alive, AND an egg is alive, THEN two live organisms combine to make a live embryo. THEREFORE, eliminating the little "jelly glob" (by any means) is actually eliminating a live embryo/human. (My Disclaimer: I'm *not* choosing sides on the abortion issue. I'm actually, anti-abortion/pro-choice, and, yes, a person can be both. I'm against abortion as a convenience or form of birth control, but I think it's up to every family to decide for themselves . . . after careful consideration. It's not my business to tell anyone what to do.)

Gun Control. In my day, people lived by the Medea creed of home protection. ("This is *my* house!") Guns were commonplace around my house and just about everywhere in our town. My father, uncles, cousins, their friends, and their friends' friends all had guns. Our neighbors had guns. The man across town had guns. The mayor owned guns, and so did city council members. To this day, I own guns, including collector guns. I have a registered gun, as well as a concealed carry permit.

When I was in my sixties, my grandson taught me how to shoot a 20-gauge shotgun. I also took a gun course where I shot everything from an old-west revolver, to pistols, to rifles, even to a bow and arrows. Plus, I'm a past member of the NRA. Needless to say, I'm comfortable around guns, and being around them was never an issue for me.

Nonetheless, I realize that many people are very uncomfortable around guns. For some people, even the very mention of them conjures up fear and loathing, and I understand that. For whatever reason that anyone has for *not* wanting to go near a gun, I respect that, and I wouldn't dare try to persuade them otherwise.

Guns can be lethal when used improperly. But for me, the *proper* use of guns is for protection.

When I was a child, I never saw my dad pull his gun on anyone. In fact, he didn't carry his gun around with him. It was only for the protection of our house and his grocery store. Neither did he ever "run home to get his gun" and bring it to an argument or fight. As a matter of fact, my dad wasn't a fighter. He was a very soft-spoken man who never raised his voice, much less argued with anyone. Also, dad kept his guns in his bedroom, and that room was off-limits to us kids. We also weren't allowed to play with a gun or even handle it without supervision.

While many may not see guns as the problem, still gun violence is, and for that reason, I believe we need some sort of gun control. The question is *what type of control* and *how* do you control guns being bought illegally? As the saying goes, "If you take guns away from people, only the criminals will have guns."

All that having been said, just because we may not be able to stop the purchase of illegal firearms, or the violent use of them by anyone, including "law-abiding citizens," that doesn't mean we shouldn't try to make our society safer. And for that, I have a four-step plan to help curve the tide of gun violence.

1. Parents teach children respect for human life.
2. Parents keep guns in a safe place.

3. Parents watch your children like a hawk and if you get a funny feeling that something is wrong, seek help for them.

4. Authorities, when a parent comes to you with a problem child or violent mate, do something! (Yeah, yeah, I know the law says this, and the law says that, and people are reluctant to act because they think they'll get sued, but we're talking about human beings, here. Surely, there's a work-around somewhere.)

Political Correctness, Sugarcoating, and Blanding
(No, I don't mean blending.)

It's a noble gesture to temper our language sometimes so we don't grossly offend people, but why do we sugarcoat everything these days? Is it so that our words don't sound bad or offensive? Don't you think it's impossible (not to mention, stressful) to innoculate every word so that we won't upset anyone? Is it feasible to think that you can "bland" everything to keep people happy and protect yourself from controversy?

I grew up in an era when everyone understood what "right and wrong" meant. Back then, people called a spade, a spade. Nowadays, people try to be so politically correct that word meanings get lost in language. You almost need a linguistics translator to help you understand.

I admit that I sometimes get sucked into the political correctness wave, too, but in my heart, I still think that calling something what it is makes conversation easier to understand and gets to the point a whole lot quicker.

Let me start with this example: We've almost erased the word "retard," and all of its variations, from our language. I wouldn't be afraid to bet that even the very sound of the word makes you cringe. So to keep from saying it over and over, let's use the term, "the 'R' word."

To be clear, I'm not saying that we ought to go back to using the "R" word to describe people with mental disabilities (and disabilities is another word that has been sugarcoated). I'm just saying that we can't change or rewrite *every* word in our language just because it sounds unpleasant to us. If so, it will lose its intended meaning. In some cases, we need the "R" word. (By the way, by definition, the "R" word simply means to delay or hold back in terms of progress, development, or accomplishment.) Without the "R" word, "flame retardant fabrics," "insect retardant rugs," "mildew retardant paints," and many other words would not exist. What would we put in their place? Flame-challenged fabric? Insect differently-abled rugs? Mildew delayed paint? Sounds silly when you hear it said like that, doesn't it?

I'm sure *you* can think of many, many other words that we've sugarcoated or blanded, but here are just a few that came to my mind:

--Handicap. "Handicapped" (which simply "means a circumstance that makes progress or success difficult") has been morphed into something barely recognizable. We changed handicapped to disabled. Then we changed disabled to challenged. Then we changed challenged to different. A person who once was handicapped – by reason of the fact that he or she encountered circumstances that impeded their progress or success – is now "differently abled." Again, I'm not advocating the return to some of our discarded language. I'm just saying that we shouldn't be so quick to change things. At the rate we're going, I wonder what "differently abled" will become in the next ten years or if we'll even have a word to put in its place.

--**He and She.** We changed "he" and "she" to "they." That's ludicrous to me! Oh, don't think I don't "get it." I understand that some people believe they were born into the wrong body or that their gender is fluid. Yes, I get that, but don't expect me to change the way I think about it. I don't believe in sex change surgeries (pardon me, "gender reassignment surgeries"). I believe that if God made you with male genitalia, keep them. If you are a man who likes men, just be a man who likes men, *not* a man who likes men, but changes to a female, who still likes men. Besides, after those surgeries, some men come out looking like ~~ugly~~ uhhhh, unappealing women, not to mention all the medications and other things they have to do to maintain their "feminine" appearance. Doesn't that sound crazy and mixed up to you? Anyway, "he" is a perfectly good word to describe a male and "she" is a perfectly good word to describe a female.

--**Man.** I admit that, in some cases, a neutral gender works. Words like "firefighter" or "police officer" fit but why can't we also use "man" and "woman" also? Why can't a *man* who fights fires be a fire*man*, or a person who polices be a police*man* or police*woman*?

--**Women Reverends**. Well, for this one, I expose my own prejudice. It's not because I don't believe women should be preachers. It's because, all my life the term "reverend" was a masculine term, and it just doesn't sound right in my ears to call a woman preacher "reverend" (although I don't know what else to call an ordained woman). Moreover, the old way of saying

"Reverend sister" to distinguish women reverends from men reverends, sounds sexist to me.

I have the same prejudice and discomfort about women wearing ministerial collars, although I myself do wear one when protocol dictates. After thinking about this topic, I guess the only thing I can say to *myself* – and others like me with the same prejudices – "We just need to get over it!"

Stand Your Ground

Let me say from the outset that I'm *in favor* of standing your ground. I think people ought to "stand their ground" to keep from being physically hurt or taken advantage of by others who would do them harm. I think stand-your-ground laws probably were meant for good but, like so many other laws meant to help, it only takes one individual to foul everything up for everyone else.

Here's how I see the *good* in standing your ground: If you're at home – minding your own business – and someone comes into your house, uninvited, you don't have to run and hide. Stand your ground and protect your property and loved ones. Likewise, if you're in your car, and someone tries to open your door and jump in, stand your ground. If you're on a bus, subway, or just walking along a city street, and thugs start pushing you around, stand your ground.

On the other hand, standing your ground does *not* mean that you follow someone down the street and shoot them in the back. Standing your ground does *not* mean that you have the right to accost someone because you think they are in the "wrong" neighborhood. And standing your ground *certainly* does *not* mean that you (or you and your friends) have the right to harm someone just because they *fought back* after *you* (or you and your friends) attacked them.

Again, standing your ground is good in some instances. No one wants to be the victim of a real threat. But I have a novel idea. What if we thought of standing our ground differently? What if, instead of thinking that standing *our* ground means impulsively and aggressively grabbing a weapon at the first sign of our *perceived* threat, we started standing our ground in *good* and *positive* ways?

- When you see social injustice, instead of joining in, stand your ground and be the voice of change.
- When you see those who cannot help themselves, stand your ground and lend a hand.
- When you see someone being abused, stand your ground and step in.
- When you see the marginalized in society (e.g., hungry, homeless, elderly, oppressed), stand your ground and help in whatever way you can.
- If someone asks you to be a part of a fraud or a scam, stand your ground and say, "No."
- If you see your peers stealing, stand your ground and don't be a part of it.
- If your friends break promises at will, stand your ground and keep yours.
- If you know people who lie or cheat, and they try to pull you into their web, stand your ground and walk away from it.
- If your peers constantly use foul language, especially language that disrespects females, stand your ground and be an example of respect.
- When people scoff at you for volunteering, helping strangers, not littering (or picking up litter), being kind, doing good deeds, going to church, etc., stand your ground. Keep it up!

- When people laugh at you for working a steady job, stand your ground. All lawful, honest work is honorable.
- When your "so called" friends tell you that you can make fast money selling drugs, stand your ground. Fast money, or illegal money, won't last very long and the end is jail time, or even worse, death.
- If your drunken friend says, "I'm okay to drive," stand your ground. Take the keys (and *definitely don't* get in the car with him/her).
- Parents, stand your ground when you tell your child "No." You know it's for their own good.

Short And To The Point:
Our Use Of Derogatory Ethnic Slurs

I grew up hearing Japanese people being called "Japs." It was commonplace in my community, around town, and in nearby cities. It was a byword for the people who bombed Pearl Harbor.

In my youth, I never thought much about the use of that word, or any other ethnic slur, for that matter. At the time, any person represented by those slurs meant nothing to me. They were just random people that I didn't know, living in random places I'd never visited, so they didn't count. In my small mind (small, both by youth and ignorance), they were always "those people over there," the ones in foreign lands.

In later years, my view of society broadened after moving to Durham. Being an adult in a large city, surrounded by education and exposure to elevated lifestyles, opened my eyes to a lot of things. That led to a deepening faith, which made me more insightful, respectful and empathetic. It totally changed my way of thinking.

For a long while, I thought that living in a diverse city of over a hundred thousand people, with universities in every direction, and a melting pot of culture, would mean that people would be more respectful and accepting of each other. However, I learned that being in a larger city only meant a larger number of the same negative attitudes toward those who are different. I didn't understand then, as I *still* don't understand now, how anyone could live next to someone, work on the same job with them – and sometimes even go to the same church – yet still belittle and disrespect them only because they look different. Wait. I take that back. I *do* understand. Ignorance and hatred produce narrow and closed minds, no matter where people live.

Nonetheless, after seeing so many things over the years, I still have hope for humankind. My hope is that we all learn to live together in peace and that I won't have to hear another story about someone being discriminated against or disrespected because of *any* difference. So this is my appeal to us all: Can we please lose words like "Wop" for Italian people, "Chinch" for Chinese people, "Japs" for Japanese people, "Rag Heads" for muslims and people from Eastern countries; "Dago" for Mediterranean people; "Redskin" for indigenous people; and "Kike" for Jewish people. (As a matter of fact, I don't even like saying the word "Jew." I prefer saying "Hebrew," or "Israelite," or at least say "Jewish person.") While we are on the subject can we stop calling all Hispanics or Latinos "Mexicans." Not all are from Mexico. Some are Spaniards (from Spain), and the words Latinos/Latinas represent people from Latin America, such as Mexico, El Salvador, Cuba, Costa Rica, Pueto Rico (pronounced Poo-et-o), the Caribbean, and many more.

Can I get down off my soapbox now?

Extremes, Extremists; Alarms, Alarmists. Hmmmm

Yes, the squeaky wheel deserves some oil, but does it have to drive the whole car? Yet that's what we do when we immediately support people who tout extreme ideas, or "sound the alarm" over anything they don't like.

I'm not saying that you should never support or oppose anything. Certainly those who witness (or are victims of) rape, abuse, child pornography, human trafficking, etc., ought to scream at the top of their lungs and sound every alarm they can find. However, sometimes people take on a cause, jump on any bandwagon, or follow others, no matter how far left or right they are, without stopping to examine the issues from all sides.

Causes, projects, movements, etc., are not inherently bad in and of themselves, but you have to admit that some people take things way too far. For example, I heard that an Alabama library flagged a children's book because the author's last name is "Gay." In my opinion, that's so extreme that it's off the charts. Should we disregard and degrade every person whose last name is Gay? Hmmmm. That's as ludicrous as advocating that every person with the last name "Gay" should change their family name. By that line of thinking, Marvin and Alberta Gay (parents of singer Marvin Gay[e]) should have denounced their names. That would also mean that U.S. politicians, Thomas and Tim Gay, and American soccer goalkeeper, Adelaide Gay should do the same. Not only that, but should we also denounce the Enola Gay, which, by the way, was named after the mother of the pilot, Colonel Paul Tibbets? Are we saying that all the hundreds, no doubt thousands, of other Gays (pardon the pun) in the world should be forgotten? Is that what the world is coming to? Is the world coming to a point where anything that anyone doesn't like will be done away with? Is that the "eutopia" (false though it may be) that we are heading toward? Again, I say, "Hmmmm."

Can you imagine being ostracized, bullied, or criticized because of your name? Oh, yes, I forgot. America has a history of that, such as what was done to mid-19th Century immigrants with names like O'Sullivan (Irish), Sabatelli (Italian), Bachurski (Polish), and Shulman (Jewish). Of course, that only includes those who came through Ellis Island. Those brought here, forcibly, or those who braved the Atlantic in small boats, or crossed southern borders, are still trying to find their place in this land of "huddled masses yearning to breathe free."

Sadly, we've taken a perfectly good, innocuous word, like "gay" and villainized it, failing to realize that the original meaning of the word meant "carefree," "cheerful," or "brightly colored," and "showy." Perhaps we should pull "gay" out of the negative and put it back in the positive.

While we're at it, why not pull some other words out of the negative and put them back to where they belong? We could start by using God's name as it was meant to be used – for praise and worship – rather than a defamed by-word tacked in front of the word "damn." To add to it, we could stop turning our noses up every time we see a rainbow flag or emblem just because a group of people in the 1970s decided to use it as their symbol of unity. After all, a rainbow is God's original symbol of an everlasting promise. The "bow" in the sky is a Covenant between God and humankind. (Genesis 9:16)

I think a good test of what is extreme is to ask ourselves a few questions. Does it benefit everyone, as a whole, or just a few? Does it cause you to pause and question whether you should be doing it, joining it, or supporting it? Does it alter your common sense? Does it splinter from mainstream society in such a way that it causes you to hide, steal, lie, cheat, hate, or in any way promote violence against another?

We have desensitized ourselves to so many other things, so why not go another step further and desensitize ourselves to *someone else's view* of who a person is or their status in life? Being around people who are different won't change who *you* are. Black won't rub off on you. Neither will gender differences, poverty, lifestyle, mental weaknesses, etc., etc, and a thousand more etcs.

Uhhhhhhh . . .

"Are you ready Kathy?" Jennifer asked. "Yes, I think so," Kathy replied.

Jennifer, a Pro-Choice advocate, was accompanying Kathy to the Cace Street Women's Clinic.

"If you're sure you're ready," Jennifer answered, "Then let's go. Our supporters are waiting to escort us in."

Even before the car rolled to a stop, other Pro-Choice advocates surrounded them to protect Kathy from the Pro-Life demonstrators gathered in front of the Clinic. Kathy hesitated for a moment, took a deep breath, then pulled the door handle.

"Let's just do it," she said and threw open the door. By now the angry Pro-Life activists had engulfed the Pro-Choice group, and Kathy and Jennifer found themselves being pushed and shoved along with the crowd. Each step carried them only inches closer to the door.

One women jumped in front of Kathy and shouted, "You're taking an innocent life!" She was quickly yanked out of the way by someone from the Pro-Choice group. Off to the side, a man dropped to his knees and began praying, "Lord forgive them for they know not what they do." In front of them another man shook his Bible angrily in the air, "God sees you and He will make you pay for what you are doing!" he shouted.

Kathy inched closer to the door. She could hear a scuffle going on behind her but didn't turn around.

Then she heard the sound of someone being dragged away. "Just ignore them," Jennifer whispered in her ear. "Just keep walking; keep moving and ignore them."

Kathy kept a steady pace. The door was just a few feet away now. Just a few short steps . . . .

Suddenly it hit her. That cold, stark reality that once she entered those doors her life would be changed forever. Then that sullen, unmistakable monster called "fear" pervaded her. It had crept upon her out of nowhere and slapped her in the face like a cold blast of arctic wind. Maybe it was the impact of the crowd, or all the stress she'd been under for the last several weeks. She didn't know what it was, but the entity shook her frame and sent shivers through her body. It brought tears to her eyes. Her knees buckled.

Jennifer felt Kathy's body sway, so she drew her closer to support her weight. "Just take it easy, Kathy. We're almost there. Just a few more steps. Just a few more . . . ."

Before she could stop her, Kathy bolted from Jennifer's grip, darted through the crowd and into the parking lot.

"All right! All right!" she screamed at the Pro-Life group. "You win!"

A loud cheer rose from the crowd. Arms lifted in the air. The man who prayed yelled, "Thank you Jesus!"

Tears streamed down Kathy's cheeks as she stood alone, encircled by astonished protesters from both sides.

"I just can't do it," Kathy began, gathering her strength. "What you say does make sense. This baby does deserve a life. I know that. I-I've known that for a long time. But I just didn't know what else to do."

"We understand honey," a woman's voice rang out from the Pro-Life group. "But . . . ."

"No you don't understand!" snapped Kathy. "You don't understand a doggone thing!"

The woman sank back in shock. "Poor child," she rationalized. "The confusion and frustration is taking its toll."

Kathy took a few steps forward, wiping the tears from her eyes. "You just don't understand," she said once more, calmly, dropping her head.

"I-I'm hear today," she began, "because I just recently found out that I have full blown AIDS, and," she continued, "there is an almost one-hundred percent chance that when my baby is born, she will have it too. And even if my baby doesn't have it, it's likely that I won't live long enough to raise my child. The doctors say that I have only a few months to live. Also, tests show that my baby has other multiple health issues, including blindness and some type of motor function problems.

Utter shock was on the faces in the Pro-Life crowd. "AIDS?" a few whispered. "Blindness," whispered another. "Cripled?" another repeated.

"I know many of you are wondering how I got AIDS," Kathy continued, "and the fact is, I don't know."

"Kathy, you don't owe these people any explanation," Jennifer cautioned her.

"I know," Kathy spoke with a sigh. "But I want to say this." She paused, then continued. "I'm not a hemophiliac or IV drug user. Neither have I engaged in risky sex. In fact, I was celibate for more than six years until about a year ago when I became serious with this baby's father. But it wasn't him, either. He's HIV negative."

Puzzled looks crept slowly across faces in the crowd. Kathy continued. "Really, I don't know how I got it. Maybe it was a blood transfusion I received while doing volunteer work overseas several years ago. Or maybe it was tainted blood in a lab accident. Or maybe I got it from my ex-husband who really was a drug user before going into rehab. Sadly, he passed away a few months ago. I don't know. And anyway who cares how I got it, right? The fact remains that I have it . . . and I'm pregnant."

Kathy drew sympathetic looks from the crowd. Some nodded in agreement. Others in apprehension. Some clung to each other. Others cried. Kathy continued.

"But you've shown me that this baby deserves a life. Even though I won't be around to watch her grow up, and even though doctors say she might not live to age 10, I'll have the comfort in knowing that I at least gave her a chance to taste life, right?"

A few unsure, cautious nods dotted the crowd. A woman in back whispered to her husband, "Do you think we're doing the right thing?" Staunch in his resolve, he whispered back, flatly, "Of course we are! People need to learn that they can't just go around destroying lives like that." Several people in the crowd drew closer to their companions, some to comfort, some thankful that it wasn't one of their children, and some speculating that some prior recklessness was finally catching up with her and this was her punishment.

Kathy gazed directly at the crowd, soliciting sympathy wherever she found it. "After seeing you all here, I know you are concerned about me, and about my baby." She drew in a strengthening breath. "I can feel the warmth and love kindling in your midst."

Pollyanna smiles criss-crossed the Pro-Life crowd. Their chests swelled with pride over their accomplishments and aspirations. And this moment – the saving of an innocent life – was the culmination of their beliefs, their goodness, and existence as a group.

Kathy went on. "I know that you must be dedicated people to come out here like this and speak out for what you believe in."

"Yes, we are," insisted one man.

"And because you believe so strongly in your cause," Kathy continued, "I know that you would do anything, given the chance, to prove the commitment of your convictions."

"That's right!" rang a voice from the crowd. Others murmured in agreement.

Kathy smiled and drew in a breath. "That's good. I thought so. I knew I could count on you. And I know my baby girl can count any one of you, too."

The crowd, suddenly knowing, grew silent. Slowly, their expressions changed from understanding and empathy, to disbelief, then to shock, and finally, to fear. Frightened whispers rose through the air. "Us?" one voice asked.

"AIDS baby?" asked another.

"She wants one of us to adopt an AIDS baby?" said one.

"Multiple illnesses and disabilities," said another.

"But she's asking for our help," someone pleaded.

"Gee, I don't know about that," lamented someone else.

Kathy took a few steps toward the crowd. "Will you be the one?" she asked the woman who had been the first to jump in front of her when she arrived at the clinic.

"Uhhhhhhh . . . I . . . uhhhhhhh," the woman stammered.

Kathy quickly turned to the man with the Bible. "And what about you sir," she pleaded.

"Yea-uh, Reverend Fawcette," came a voice from the crowd. "You and Mrs. Fawcette don't have any children. Maybe this is God's way of blessing you with a child."

"Well. Yes, but . . . . I mean, no. I mean, I don't think this is what God had in mind," Reverend Fawcette stammered.

Kathy turned, this time to a couple. "Please. Won't you take my baby? You look like decent, kind people."

"Well we are. That is, we try to be. But we've got four other children and we wouldn't want them to . . . uh . . . I'm sorry."

"I see," Kathy replied and dropped her head. "I see very well, and I understand perfectly. It's easy to point a finger at someone else as long as the shoe isn't on your foot." With that, she pushed her way back through the crowd and entered the building.

The End Is Near??

The scene: *A man walks down a busy street in Anycity, USA. We don't know his name, so let's call him Jack.*

Jack pulls his trench coat closer around his neck and tucks his head lower inside the collar. Jack's gait is even and steady. He never looks up as he plods angrily along the busy sidewalk.

The camera follows Jack as he crosses Elm Street and makes a right on Oak. Just as he rounds the corner, suddenly a crazed man jumps out of the shadows in front of him. Hair stringy and dirty, eyes bulging and bloodshot, the camera can't help but pick up the man's glaring eyes, now staring directly into its lens. Without warning he turns to Jack and yells, "The end is near!"

Unscathed by the attack, Jack angrily pushes past the man. "Get out of my way, you raging lunatic!" he yells back. Unphased, the man continues down the street yelling, "The end is near! The end is near!"

This same scene is often played out in movies, commercials and even livestreams. If encountering a crazed man on the street, most people would likely do as Jack did: write the man off as a raging lunatic, a schizophrenic out of touch with reality. But what if the end is actually near and the man is not a lunatic? What if he has actually received a vision from God, but because of his slovenly appearance no one takes him seriously?

I don't think we'd blame anyone for ignoring a crazy-looking, sloppily dressed person, but what about one who is fashionably and stylishly dressed, bringing a message of hope and redemption? Would they be ignored and their message get lost in disbelief, too?

Many prophets of old received Heavenly messages, and I dare say that people still see visions and receive prophecies today. Yet peoples' disbelief in those Heavenly messages has not changed. Today, just as in olden times, some believe and some don't. Scoffers still exist and Heavenly messages still fall on deaf and/or skeptical ears.

No doubt people laughed at Noah the entire 100+ years it took him to build the ark, but their *dis*belief didn't stop the rain from coming. (Genesis 6:1-8; Matthew 24:38) People didn't believe Old Testament prophets like Jeremiah (Jer. 7), or Micah, and not even New Testament writers like Matthew or Timothy, and especially the Revelation of John. Thousands of years ago, these disciples all told of things to come, things that are actually happening today. (Matthew 24; 2 Timothy 3; Revelation).

It's easy to shrug and say, "That was hundreds of years ago. We've heard all those stories before . . . ." (which, by the way, is another Scripture). But even if you don't believe the old prophets, what about those of modern times? What about Billy Graham, Martin Luther King, Jr., and Norman Vincent Peale? We also can't leave out Juanita Bynum, D. James Kennedy, Bernice King, and Charles Stanley to name a few more. Say what you want about any of them, their prophetic warnings, and most importantly, their messages of hope and reconciliation came through in their sermons.

In our youth, even if we didn't hear their sermons, our parents and grandparents made sure we heard the Word. Although sometimes slightly skewed, the truth still emerged from their Biblical quotes. My dad would say, "The Bible says, before the end of time, you won't be able to tell the winter from the summer except by the budding of the trees." Even though I searched extensively and never found that particular quote in the Bible, over the years I've noticed that the prophecy seems to be coming true. There have been colder springs and warmer winters. As a matter of fact, there have been many recorded snowstorms and ice storms in April, well after trees have bloomed. Also, there have been some days in December so hot that people wore summer clothes.

Another prophetic memory that I have dates back to 1973. A co-worker told me that there would come a day when money would be no good because people wouldn't accept it. I viewed his prediction with a little skepticism while at the same time I halfheartedly believed. His prediction came flooding back this past June while visiting family in Atlanta. It blew my mind when my family and I walked into a popular restaurant and saw a sign in the window that read, "credit cards only."

My co-worker also talked of a one-world government and one-world monetary system, another prediction that I half scoffed at because it seemed so far-fetched and unbelievable at the time. Yet, on January 1, 1999, the Euro came into effect and by 2002, twelve European countries changed their currency to the Euro.

I really started to take note of those earlier predictions when I noticed all the banks that have folded or merged in recent years. I also noticed the number of new credit card companies that have sprung up. On top of that, the majority of them are not even brick-and-mortar companies. They are "financial technology companies," which in my book simply means that they only exist in the millions of zeros, ones, and algorithms that make up internet/computer language.

As we think about financial institutions and electronic conveniences, I ask you, when was the last time you set foot in a bank? Remember when Friday was check-cashing day? Remember when you sat in front of a bank employee and ordered checks? As a matter of fact, do people even write checks anymore? Every time I see one of those "dinosaurs" my jaw drops and I marvel at the sight.

Don't get me wrong. The word "dinosaur" applies to me too. I have a checkbook somewhere in my house, and I keep a couple of "just-in-case" checks in my wallet. Still, I enjoy modern conveniences like everyone else. I bank online, order groceries online, and a certain online warehouse gets my money for just about everything else. However, while I'm enjoying all the conveniences that this 21st Century has to offer, I keep those Biblical predictions in mind.

Aside from other predictions, such as diseases, pestilence, and high prices, the predictions that worry me most are the ones about wars, lack of natural love, and the anti-Christ. Scoff if you will, but haven't you noticed the number and frequency of wars and scrimmages happening, and some of them in the most unlikely places? (Wars – I mind you – do not necessarily mean global conflicts.) The lack of "natural love," to me, is not about same-sex relationships. It's about the fact that people seem so cold toward each other. Those natural instincts like respect, caring, empathy and love seem to be lost nowadays. Notice how people are more grumpy, hateful, fearful and mistrustful?

So far as the anti-Christ is concerned, keep a close watch on elections and other strategic political moves around the world. According to the Bible, the anti-Christ will *seem* to be righteous and people will follow him blindly and believe everything he says, no matter how far-fetched it is. The anti-Christ will be merciless, wielding an iron fist and forcing his way into being a dictator. That person will deceive many. That person will set up a one-world government. That person will control everything, including what people do and say, and will do away with anyone who opposes him. That person will put a mark on people's foreheads (not necessarily a visible, physical mark, but perhaps brainwashing them into believing in an ideology and marking them with a symbol of that ideology).

One last thing that sticks out in my mind is something that my cousin said a long time ago. He cautioned us to learn as many Scriptures as possible because one day even the Bible would be taken from us. As far-fetched as it seemed then, it's not so unbelievable now. Watch out for the smallest, subtlest changes in religion. They may result in bigger things down the road. Will our freedom of religion be taken away? Is a dictatorship coming to America? If so, what will be the result?

Is the end near? No one knows for sure, but if I were you, I wouldn't take a bet on it *not* happening soon. All we can do is stay woke, keep fighting for a brighter future, and keep looking up.

Who Are The Five People You Think You'll Meet In Heaven?

In 2003, Mitch Albom wrote a book called *The Five People You Meet In Heaven.* The basic point of his book is that everyone has purpose and the people we meet influence us in some way. The story is told from the viewpoint of Eddie, who dies, goes to Heaven and meets five people whose life he touched, or who touched his life when he was alive. This true story that I'm about to tell to you is about a teacher who had assigned Albom's book to her English class. For anonymity, I'll call them Jane Doe and Sally Smith.

Jane and Sally shared a large classroom in the Exceptional Children's Department of a local high school. Actually, the "classroom" was a 24'x40' mobile unit (a trailer, in other words). Mobile units were the school district's answer to overcrowding. Jane's and Sally's schedules were arranged so that while one was teaching the other had a planning period.

Jane and Sally happened to be same-gender-loving females (not in a relationship with each other). Jane is white and Sally is black.

While Sally sat on the far end of the classroom preparing for her next class, Jane was conducting a discussion of Albom's book with her students. In the middle of the discussion, Jane called out across the classroom, "Ms. Smith, who do you think will be the five people you'll meet in Heaven?"

Having never read Albom's book, Sally *assumed* it was about people being surprised when they got to Heaven and saw folks they never thought would make it. She assumed the main character arrived in Heaven and met people like the hateful old neighbor or the wino on the corner, or the prostitute that everyone knew. So, without skipping a beat, Sally quipped, jokingly, "Well, I don't know who the *five* people will be, but *two* of them will be Jesse Helms and Jerry Falwell."

Jane's response was automatic and uncontrollable. She roared with laughter, leaving her students stunned and confused, for they didn't get the joke . . . but I hope you do.

(The punchline comes from the fact that there was a time when Jesse Helms spued his racist and sexist ideologies freely over the airwaves and Jerry Falwell did the same, smathered with his disdain for homosexuality. But the joke loses its flavor if the punchline has to be explained.)

A Band Of Angels Comin' After Me

This "cutesy" little fictional tale is an excerpt from Kinfolks and Other Unrelated Relatives, one of my early unpublished manuscripts. Given the current social and political climate of extremism in America today, this felt like the perfect time to include it in Truly Grounded.)

The year was 2026, or some other time in the not-so-distant future. The setting: Purity High School auditorium, 7:30 PM. The event: a town meeting to discuss the sale and storage of obscene literature in the local bookstore. The players: Shawn Broquer, a book salesman; John Deller, the bookstore owner; and Hillery Pace, the CEO of a New York publishing company.

A shadowy figure stands silently in back of the auditorium, scanning the standing-room-only crowd, eyes stopping momentarily on a few people known only through vague introductions. The shadow slowly inches into the light, revealing a tall, slender, dark-haired man. It was Shawn Broque, and he was already ten minutes late for the Board of Aldermen meeting. Nonetheless, he took the time to take a deep breath and gain his composure.

Ordinarily, Purity citizens would have treated Shawn warmly whenever he was in town, but tonight they circled him like hungry sharks. Shawn wondered how things could have turned so sour so quickly, and over nothing. Yet, there he was, along with Hillery and John, all thrown together only because of the similarity of their professions. The charge: "conspiring to subvert the innocence of minors," a made-up charge supported by an imaginary city ordinance. It all seemed so surreal, yet scary at the same time. To think that people could be so close-minded in this age! As Shawn stood there in the doorway, his mind drifted back to the events that led up to this night.

Shawn had been selling books in Purity since the 1960s. Back then, the town was called Freedom, an idyllic community of about one-thousand people. Ten miles to the North of Freedom was Haven, another idyllic little town, rustic, calm, peaceful, almost identical in amenities to Freedom, yet Freedom was where everyone wanted to be. Drawn by its many tennis courts, baseball fields, an art museum, a civic center, a movie theater, outdoor swimming pools, and churches of various denominations, Freedom attracted people from all walks of life, and all parts of the country. It was a wonderful place to live, grow and raise a family. In fact, Freedom had been voted the best "all-around city in the South" for three years straight.

Over the years, though, subtle changes took place in Freedom. It started in the early 1980s when the conservative right trend started sweeping across the nation. As more towns began to form morality groups, Freedom soon got caught up in the fray. They fought to end social degradation, "the liberal agenda" as they called it. They also railed against anything they considered to be moral deviance. Before long, a few people got together and formed their own morality group, their main displeasure being – as they put it – that the town "put too much emphasis on sports and other secular activities that did nothing to uplift and stimulate the soul." The group's name, "The Association of Reformed Righteousness" (aka,

T.A.R.R. (thankfully, minus the feathers)). Like an invasive cancer, they inserted as many members as possible into every governmental office in town.

As word got out about T.A.R.R's views, other people with similar interests moved in, and by the late 1980s T.A.R.R. had swelled to engulf over half the population. Before long, the whole complexion of Freedom changed, and eventually, the remaining original residents either moved to Haven or became splinter groups, dispersed on the outskirts of the city. In a rapid chain of events, Freedom metamorphosized and isolated itself from every other city around. Then the inevitable happened. Town officials voted to change Freedom's name to Purity to reflect what they said was its "pure and virtuous" image. In time, Shawn, Hillery, and John somehow got swept into the lunacy, and they were branded as promoters of "garbage literature."

At first, Shawn scoffed at the rumors and allegations, but when he heard that T.A.R.R. had set out to destroy his credibility in other cities and stage an outright boycott of his company, he started to take them very seriously. He still couldn't believe how something so simple as selling books could have escalated into an all-out war. "How had it all come down to this?" he thought. "They are threatening to destroy the very principles on which this country was founded."

Memories of those early days remained fresh in Shawn's mind as he walked down the narrow aisle. The tension in the air was unmistakable. Angry whispers and icy stares made the hairs on the back of his neck stand on end. Somehow he felt less like a grown man of sixty and more like a child found stealing cookies from the cookie jar. He sighed as he slid into his assigned seat – front row, center – next to Hillery and John.

The small, dark circles under John's eyes bore tell-tale signs of too many long nights without sleep and too many stressful days without relief. By contrast, Hillery looked fresh and confident. She fidgeted impatiently with the tablet on her lap, checked her watch repeatedly, then leaned over and whispered in her lawyer's ear. Ordinarily, she would have sent her secretary or allowed her lawyer to handle the matter, but this time she made the trip from New York herself intrigued by "those local yokels," she had called them.

Suddenly the lights went up and applause rang out when the Board members filed in and sat at the large conference table in the center of the stage. Led by Chairman I.M. Annaz, they all took their prospective seats. I.M., of course, flopped down in the center chair. "Let's all come to orduh," he started. "Come to orduh! Hey you, they-uh. In the back. Stop talkin'! It's time fuh owuh meetin' to begin, but befo' we go eny futhuh, Revern Smiff will lead us in pryuh."

A silver-haired man at the end of the table struggled to his feet. His large belly hovered over the waistband of his pants like a boulder teetering on the edge of a cliff. He wobbled to the podium, shoes squeaking with each step. Smoothing back his thinning hair, he began, his voice that thundering across the room.
"Oh Lawd . . .."

After two minutes of "thank-yous" for various blessings, three minutes of asking forgiveness for having to call the meeting in the first place, he finally ended with, "Knowing that we are only trying to do your righteous will and purge iniquity from the land, we ask that you be with us. Amen."

"Thank you, Revern Smiff, for such a fine pryuh," I.M. injected. Then he pulled one of the books from the stack in the center of the table, holding it so loosely by its spine that it almost slipped from his hand. Shawn whispered to John, "It's just a book. Not a deadly serpent," and they both snickered.

I.M. took a deep breath and began. "As y'all know, we ah he-uh ta-nīte tuh 'xamine these three peopul who have been distributin' obscene matearul." He lifted the book high over his head and shook it vigorously in the air. "And I hol-ol-ld in my hand one such book! It wuz pub-lished by Ms. Pace's cumpn, sold by Mr. Broquer an' stocked by Mr. Delluh!!" His voice trailed off in a low, throaty growl that would have made even the best televangelist green with envy.

The book fell to the table with a loud thud as I.M. walked to the edge of the stage. "If y'all will, ladies and gentlemen, turn to page 67 of the sample matearuls y'all have been given." The rustle of paper filled the air, replaced quickly by loud gasps that rippled across the room. I.M. glared directly at Shawn and his companions. "Do y'all three unduhstand why this awdience is so upset?"

"But we didn't write any of this," Shawn protested. "And besides, what's wrong with it?"

I.M. flushed red and took two awkward steps backwards. "Well let me explane it to you, Broquer," he began. "To those of us who still buleevve in inna-

cents and tradish-nal values, we don't wont ow-uh
children's minds por-suned by garbage like this."

"Garbage?!" Shawn exploded. "I grew up on poems
like these. What's wrong with you people!? They're
just simple nursery rhymes!"

Gasps and boos filled the building. I.M. struggled
to keep his composure. "Well, jus' let me try agin,
Broquer, to explane just what is wrong wit' this stuff
yew seem tuh thank is 'all right.' Let's just staaht with
the first line." I.M. flipped the page and began reading,
"Mary had a little lamb . . .."

"So?" Shawn cut in.

"*So*, Mr. Broquer! In the fuhst place, the wud 'had'
signuhfies 'birth,' and we don't wont ouwah young
chidren askin' questions about such subjects befo they
ahh ready. And in the second place . . . ." I.M. paused.
The blood left his face. "It's almost too disgustin' for
me tuh say," he stammered, drawing in a deep breath.
"In the secund place, the wud 'had', folluhed by the
wud 'lamb', implies that she . . . that . . . uh . . . had sex
. . . uh . . . intuhcourse with a sheep! That beastiality,
Broquer!"

"Oh God!" Shawn yelled in disgust. "You silly,
backwards, narrowminded people are misunderstanding
the whole thing. You people are crazy. You're . . . ."

Before Shawn could say another word, I.M.
bellowed, "That's anuf of that blasphemy! How dare
you take thuh Lowed's name in vain!"

Now there's something to be said about adreneline.
When adreneline takes over, you can suddenly do
things that you otherwise would not be able to do, and
I.M. was full of adreneline. Before anyone could stop

him, he jumped from the stage, grabbed Shawn by the collar and began pummelling him with fists of fury. It took four men to subdue I.M., giving Shawn the opportunity to wrestle free, leaving shreds of his shirt behind. In the fray, one of the men blurted, "You three had better get outa here, fast!"

John and Shawn ran to their cars and sped off. Hillery jumped into her limosine, locked the doors and yelled to her driver, "Drive! You fool! Get me out of here. Fast!"

People streamed from the auditorium in hot pursuit, only to be met by the odor of gas fumes and burnt rubber. But the loss of their prey didn't end the hunt. Instead, it set off a maelstorm in the crowd which, by now, was fueled by rage and set on revenge. They turned first to Deller's bookstore, and in a mad, ravenous frenzy, they pulled books from the shelves and ripped them to shreds. *Sleeping Beauty* and *Macbeth* were among the first to go because of their depiction of witches and magic potions. *Robin Hood* and books containing rhymes like "Tom Tom the Piper's Son" met a similar fate because they glorified the life of crime. They even ripped open recorded materials, smashed computers, and broke vintage cassettes and albums.

The purge was on. With piranha-like precision, they stripped every shelf to the bare walls. Then with the intensity of a Category 5 tornado, they swept through the town, raiding people's houses and pulling books from bookcases and attics, reading materials that most of the homeowners had long since forgotten they still owned.

Somewhere in the heat of rage, somebody got the idea of burning all the confiscated contraband in the town square. It would be a bonfire, they said, for "literary cleansing." Before they knew it, the heap had grown to over fifty feet wide and two stories high. It produced a glorious blaze indeed, that burned, and burned, and burned.

Early the next morning, a strange news story broke the airwaves:

This is Tom Priess reporting to you live from what used to be the picturesque little town of Purity. What a tragedy that unfolded here last night. The whole town almost burned to the ground in a bizarre book-burning incident. Only a few houses and businesses remain standing today.

Details are sketchy at this time but apparently the blaze started in the town square, then accidentally ignited some nearby buildings and spread quickly to area homes. With limited resources to contain the blaze, there was little that townspeople could do.

So Purity, the town that had dubbed itself "The Island of Light in a Sea of Darkness" is no more. Its people are without anywhere to sleep tonight and the governor is making an appeal on their behalf to neighboring towns for shelter.

Tom ended his report, signed off, and headed to his news van for a short break. Within minutes the telephone rang. The voice on the other end sounded confident and reassuring. "Hello? This is the Mayor of Haven."

"Yes?" Tom responded, listening with intrigue.

"Listen," the Mayor continued, "We heard your story, the one about the people from Purity. And we want to let you know that we'll take 'em in. We don't have an over abundance of resources, but we'd be glad to share what we have. We'll find a way."

Tom was ecstatic when he burst from his trailer. He was almost out of breath by the time he reached a group of T.A.R.R. members standing with Mayor-elect Gilford Payne.

"Hey, I j-just got a call from the Mayor of Haven," Tom cut in. "Great news! They said they'd be glad to take you all in. They'll even send buses to pick you up."

The mayor stared blankly at Tom before finally speaking, half-heartedly, "Well, thank you for the information, son," and without another word, he turned back to the group, and there, in the smoldering ashes, they held a meeting. Puzzled, Tom turned and walked away. "Why would they even have to think about anything?" he thought. "I just brought them the greatest news of their lives, right now, and they hold a meeting? Geez!"

In a few minutes, Mayor-elect Payne emerged from the group.

"Hey there, Mr. Priess, wait." Tom turned to meet Payne's stern gaze. "We've thought it over and discussed it, and we've come to a unanimous decision," he continued, as if preparing to make a grand speech. "Tell the people of Haven that we really appreciate their offer, but we think it best that we stay right here where we are. We're going to start rebuilding immediately."

Tom was knocked off his feet by their cavalier attitude. "But you'll need somewhere to stay while you're rebuilding," he insisted.

"Yes. We know," Payne answered. But we have a few buildings and some old warehouses still standing. We'll just hafta bunch up. Ya see, young fella, we're a unique group of people and we stand behind what we believe in. Other people who don't hold our same beliefs might try to taint our folks' minds. It'll cause a lot of confusion."

Shocked and bewildered, Tom shook his head and walked away.

Now this story just goes to show you that some people think they're so right that even Haven isn't good enough for them.

PART IV: FACING CHALLENGING QUESTIONS

Down through the years, my life experiences have taught me a lot. They have slowly moved me from a narrowminded, pessimistic thinker, to one who embraces eclectic ideals. They brought me out of my shell and moved me closer to experiencing life on a different, more elevated, level.

Facing challenges in life helps us break through our steel-encased façades that hide us from others. Once we face some of the challenges in life, and lift the façade, we gain a broader view of our place in the world.

We are challenged to ask questions and seek answers to those questions by looking beyond our preset mentality and take an inverted view of what we think we already know. In doing so, we might be pleasantly surprised at what we find.

The Illegal Immigrants: A "What If" Short Story

Two men sat in their favorite spot under a grove of oak trees, preparing their tools for fishing. In a few minutes, a certain group of people walked past, which sparked a conversation between the two men.

Man 1: "I get so sick and tired of seeing them in this country."

Man 2: "Yeah, me too. We used to own all of this land. Now they come here, all bunched up together, messing up everything, using our precious resources."

Man 1: "Yeah, and they're not like us either. They don't have the same values as we do, and they don't know how to act. Always tearing up things. No respect for us and what we stand for."

Man 2: "I wish everybody in this country had stuck together from the beginning. Then we wouldn't have this problem. But those weaklings farther up north gave in. Now look what we got. One big mess! And another thing. How do they come over here with nothing, and get more than we can get? If it wasn't for us, they'd starve to death."

Man 1: "Yep. And if our people in the border towns and some of the other leaders hadn't been so weak, we would still have our country to ourselves. I'd like to know the name of that first guy who sold them a piece of land! I'd give him a piece of my mind. Didn't he know that if you give in to one, you suddenly got a whole slew of 'em."

Man 2: "Not only that, but they keep having babies and spreading all over this land like wildfire. And I heard they steal and carry all kinds of diseases, and . . ..

Awwww, I guess there's no sense in fussin' about it now. What's done is done."

The men finish their work, start packing up everything, and head for home.

Man 1: "Nen naush mohtompog." (roughly, "I'll see you tomorrow" in the Algonquian language)

Man 2: "Wunnegen." ("Good" in the Algonquian language)

Oh, by the way, I deliberately didn't tell you that the lines of dialogue were written in English for ease of reading. Also, in case you didn't get the punchline, try imagining the setting to be in the 1700s, Virginia, Algonquian (Indian) territory.

A True Story (by Eric Fuller)

When Eric told me this story, it made me sad. Why
are we so quick to forget where we came from and how
we were treated? Why do we pick on others, or think
we have the right to do so? Why not remember how we
once were abused, and instead of passing on the abuse
to someone else, try to show compassion for others?

> *I was riding home on a bus one day and when
> the bus stopped, a Hispanic woman got on with two
> infants. One looked to be about three years old and
> the other was in a stroller. In a few minutes, I heard
> a voice behind me say, "I can't stand those people.
> They come over here and take our jobs; they throw
> trash everywhere and pee on everything. They're
> just not like us."*
>
> *I turned around, fully expecting to see a
> disgruntled white man. To my surprise, it was a
> black man spewing hatred. I said, "Hey, wait a
> minute, man. Have you forgotten that it's the same
> thing white people used to say about us less than
> twenty years ago? How can you turn right around
> and say the same thing about somebody else?"*

What Happened to My Name?

Who keeps changing our nomenclature!!?? Why did "they" (the proverbial "they") feel the need to change it, and more importantly, why do we all keep going along with it? It's as if we are still under bondage, being pressed into loss of identity or, more specifically, pressed into maintaining identity separation. We went from nigger (which I agree we should have gotten rid of a long time ago), to negro, to colored, to black, and finally, to African-American in 1988. All due respect to Rev. Jesse Jackson for trying to find a name that more closely represented us as a people, but this is not an argument against his effort to promote awareness and respect for who we are. In fact, the idea of globally defining "us" started long before 1988. But my question is why do we keep changing?

James Brown said, "Say it loud, "I'm Black, and I'm proud!" And with that, it was finally "okay" to be black. What!? I've been black all my seventy-seven years and black is all that I can be. I admit, I wasn't so satisfied, years ago, with the word "negro" because, for me, it was too close to "nigger." Even though derivatives of it mean black in many languages (e.g., Spanish, Italian, French), it was too easy for some people to slip into using "nigger" ("nigress," for females).

For me, the old classification, "colored," more closely describes who I am because I am a person *of color*, which is defined as having or possessing color. Even at that, I refuse to use the word "colored" (except in "NAACP") because of my own history of living during the Jim Crow era and seeing "Colored" posted above water fountains, bathrooms, entry doors, etc. Yes, "person of color," seems like a better fit to me because it connotes being black, and black is the embodiment of *all* colors (except for white, of course, which is the *absence* of color). I use "person of color" in certain settings, but mostly, "Black," for ease of conversation. I am a person of color, who is of African ancestry and, thus, a Black woman by virtue of the fact black people came from Africa.

In the final analysis, I guess what a person calls themselves is a personal choice, but rather than forcing people to choose, I think the bigger fight ought to be changing the little blocks on applications and other forms. When I was a young job-seeker, the imp inside me wanted to mark "white" or some other ethnic group. Sometimes I wanted to draw a little box and write "person" next to it, but since that would have greatly reduced my chances of getting a job, I restrained myself.

Before I leave, I have an additional, different question: Why do we insist that every race or ethnic group in America contain "American" at the end? African-American. Mexican-American. Arab-American. Japanese-American. Chinese-American. Italian-American. To me, they all have a tone of labeling, separating, and identifying those who are *not* of European descent in a country that was stolen from natives in the first place. And now even the indigenous people of this land have been renamed Native-Americans!

Labeling

We need labels for cans, packages, garments, and such. But why do we label people or things that are not ours to label?

For example, why do we say "white folks' music" or "black folks' music," or any other cultural music? Music existed in nature eons before mankind came on the scene? Long before humans thought it was their brilliance that named the sounds, birds were already singing C-sharps and B-flats. Also, trees were swishing, elk were beating out rhythms, and fish were gurgling, centuries before we developed the instruments to copy them. So why, when we hear country music, some say, "That's white folks music?" Why, when we hear soul, doo-wop or beat boxing, we classify it as "black folks music?" I'm black and I love country music. I also love folk, rhythm and blues, jazz, gospel, symphony and many other genres. Music doesn't follow a color or race. It's what appeals to individual tastes.

We do the same thing with food. Why do we say Chinese food, rather than simply naming the food? Why not say shrimp fried rice, or beef and broccoli, or kung pao chicken? Is it so hard to say, "I have a taste for a taco from Cafe Gabriela, or a burrito from Eduardo's Grill," rather than saying, "I have a taste for some Mexican food?

The same goes for people identifiers. I was in the check-out line one day when a woman, two-customers behind me, was talking to her friend with her cell phone on speaker. Everyone in line could hear their conversation but no one reacted at first. In a minute, the woman's friend said something funny and we all chuckled quietly, except the young man who was standing directly behind me, turned around. That's when the woman said to her friend, "This white boy is laughing at what you said." Why couldn't she have simply said, "This gentleman laughed at what you said."?

Labeling pops up everywhere. One day, I witnessed a theft and I called to report it. The dispatcher said, "Can you describe the person?" But before I could give her a full description (e.g., clothes, hair color, body build, age, vehicle), she added, "Was he black, white, Mexican?"

Of course, I could go on and on, but you get the picture. But before you get mad at me, let me defend myself (or perhaps I should say, redeem myself). I have a confession to make. After giving *you* a hard time about labels, I confess that *I* sometimes fall into the same trap, especially when it comes to food. Like you, I may say, "My taste buds are calling for Italian tonight." I also label some mail as "junk" mail, some behavior as "low class," and some people as "scuzzy." (Hmmmm. Does scuzzy fall into the category of behaviors, as well?)

When it boils down to it, I guess we all are guilty of using labels from time to time, and this little conversation probably hasn't diverted anyone from doing so (including me). Hopefully, though, it has raised our awareness a bit, and at least has gotten us to think about how, when, and why we use them.

The Race Card

I don't believe in playing "the race card." Don't get me wrong. I'm not so naïve as to ignore the abject racial injustice in this country, but I refuse to use race as a ploy to gain sympathy or take advantage of any situation.

It's easy to blame race as a factor when a minority is overlooked for a job. By the same token, others may say that the *only* reason a person was picked for a certain position is *because* of their race. Even though race could very well be at issue in either case, my point is that race should not be used as a crutch or an excuse. (Hold on. Before you get all up in arms at me, put your lips back in, unfurrow your brow, and read on, please.)

The number one reason I don't believe in using the race card is that I was raised to believe that a person makes his or her own destiny. My parents taught us to be independent, never ask for a handout, and work for what we needed and wanted. Some call it the old "pull yourself up by your bootstraps" way of thinking.

Another reason that I don't use the race card is that I never saw my blackness as a barrier to *anything*. I never viewed myself as being Black, and more particularly, a *Black* woman. (Wait. Again, before you go jumping to conclusions, hear me out.) Growing up, I always saw myself as merely a person, someone just trying to make a living and carve a niche in society. I never believed that I was held back because of anything less than my lack of trying or taking opportunities as they came my way. I never saw my color as a factor in anything that I did or anywhere I went. I always believed that respect, kindness, and "niceness" were the keys to getting what I needed.

Sadly (or inevitably), that Pollyanna viewpoint changed after I aged and matured, and saw things that I could no longer ignore. It also changed when I began to educate myself about historical, systemic racism and finally woke up to the atrocities enacted against Black men. It changed when the world encroached on my idyllic view of society. But mostly, it all changed when I read – and saw – historical documentaries about the ongoing dehumanization of Black men, women, and even worse, children.

I was fine as long as my mind saw the world through rose-colored glasses, but when the filth of the world broke those lenses and pushed all of its dirtiness into my eyes, I could no longer ignore the fact that I was not just a person living in America, but I was a *Black* person in America, and more specifically a *Black woman*, living in America.

Lens shattered, glasses broken, and reality, like sandy grit flew into my eyes. Then, I began to recalled all the games that Black women used to play just to survive. On one hand, they had to act "nice" just to get along, but if they were too nice they were exploited. Some were exploited for their beauty, and others were mistreated for not being beautiful enough. Some found a little solace in acting meek, but those who stood up for themselves were hated. They were hated by men who wanted them to be subservient, and hated by women who lived in their shadow. Some were railed upon for being weak, yet expected to carry the entire load.

Regardless of how much I tried to neutralize my thinking, eventually I had to admit that as a Black woman, my blackness was a source of disdain on one end of the spectrum, and simply being tolerated or allowed on the other. Why is that? Why can't I (and by "*I*," I mean *we*) ever rise above the level of being just tolerated or allowed?

Hated. Tolerated. Allowed. Whatever Black women face, goes double for Black men. In some areas (yes, even in this 21st Century), and in some people's eyes, a fifty-year-old Black man is still a "boy." He must keep his head down and not make eye contact. He must keep his hands where they can be seen at all times. He cannot make any sudden moves or act in a threatening manner. Yet *any* mannerism at all may be seen as threatening, depending on who is in the "victim" role at any given time. He must be polite, stop when he is told, and not ask questions. When he is asked questions, his answer must be "Yes suh" or "No suh." Nothing else. And after all that, there's still no guarantee that he won't come home in a body bag, *if* he comes home at all.

Some people don't understand that those born in European countries (Spain, Italy, England, etc.) are either white, or automatically accepted into a white society when they come to America. They instinctively get a free pass. But I/we cannot pass for anything else but Black (nor would we want to). I/we cannot erase our black skin (nor do I/we want to). I/we cannot smooth out my/our extremely coarse, kinky hair (nor do I/we want to). I/we cannot change my/our race or skin color. When you see me/us, the first thing you see is my/our blackness. It's always "in your face."

After everything that is done to make us invisible, we should not stand for it. The more that some factions in America try to erase us, we should stand out like indelible ink and refuse to go away.

But there's also the other side of blackness. Unfortunately (or sadly), there are some Black people who believe that America is actually *white* America. They feel that they have no part in "these United States." They refuse to sing, stand for, or acknowledge the Star Spangled Banner as their anthem. They will not repeat the Pledge of Allegiance. They will not vote. Believe me, I get it. It's hard to turn your back on slavery and racism. It's hard to look at the pictures of "strange fruit" hanging from Southern trees and not get angry, mortified and sick. But here's another thought: If we give in to the notion that *we* are *not* a part of America, then we nullify Langston Hughes' poem, *I, Too*. We turn a blind eye to the last line that reads, "I, too, am America." We also invalidate all the hard work that Black people did in building this country. We disregard the building of skyscrapers, mapping cities, inventing products and machinery, working in mines and assembly lines, harvesting raw materials, designing and making clothes, and the list goes on and on. No, ladies and gentlemen, I'm not going to just roll over and give away *my* part in America. I'm going to cut myself a big ole slice of the pie, sit down at Uncle Sam's table, and eat it with pride, pride in the labors of my father and mother, and their parents, and all those before them. I'll take pride in the kings and queens;

princes and princesses; architects and engineers; craftspeople, designers, artists, and the endless list of those who were forced into servitude here (and that's only the ones who survived the middle passage). Their survival left us a legacy of ingenuity, perseverance, resourcefulness, honor, integrity, dignity, and so much more.

Yes, it's easy to sit back and say, "This is not *my* America; it's *their* America," but every time we say that *or believe* that, we make those very words true. Every time we fail to take part in something *in* America, we spill drops of our ancestors' **blood**. Every time we fail to stand up for our own rights, we disavow the **sweat** of their brow that built this country. Every time we fail to step into opportunities that come our way, we allow their **tears** to fall in vain.

For me, I've come to realize that my view of who we are and how we fit in the world, is a series of circles and steps. We eventually come full circle in age, maturity, thought processes, and spirituality, and when the end of one circle connects to its beginning, we then understand things that we've already learned, and that understanding then gives us the power to step up to change and begin the next learning circle. The more we learn and grow, the more we come to know ourselves (i.e., who we *truly* are). We learn that no matter what *others* think of us, no matter what little box they try to fit us into, no matter how they try to degrade, demean, or in any other way, delete us, we don't have to be defined by anyone else's definition of who we are. We must be our *own* advocates. We must not look down on ourselves. Hand up, yes. Handout, no. I may need help, but I'm not helpless. I am a strong, independent, self-reliant, resilient Black woman. And that's why I *still* do not play the race card.

(This piece is in honor and memory of my grandmother, born in 1886, the daughter of an enslaved woman, born circa 1862.)

Scary, Archaic Words

You might already know that some of the slang (much of it derogatory) we use today comes from words that originally meant something entirely different. I'm not advocating that we resurrect any archaic words, but we may find it interesting (even a bit humorous) if we look back at their original meaning.

Ass. Until the 1800s the word "ass" was defined as a beast of burden, a stubborn, dimwitted animal. Then someone (many say it was Noah Webster) took the word "arse" (which means buttocks), removed the "r" and somehow the word denigrated into its many uses today. (*Quora.com*)

Dyke (also spelled dike). A long wall or embankment, built to prevent flooding from the sea. It's also defined as a low wall or earthwork serving as a boundary or defense; a causeway; a ditch or watercourse. Remember the story of the little Dutch boy who saves his country by putting his finger in a leaking dike/dyke? The boy stayed there all night, in spite of the cold, until the villagers found him and repaired the dyke (wall).

Faggot. A faggot is a bundle of sticks, not a homosexual man. By the way, when we use the term homosexual, aren't we really saying sexual man, and aren't all of us humans sexual beings? I'm just sayin'. (Homo = man (as in homo sapien). Sexual = the instincts, physiological processes, and activities connected with physical attraction. Then homosexual means sexual man. To be clear, I am not arguing the morality of homosexuality. I'm simply saying that we sometimes unwittingly pick up words, names, causes, etc., without reason.

Fairy. Fairy comes from the old French word faerie, which itself is constructed from fae (a word for a supernatural being in old English) and the suffix "erie" (in English: "ery"). So when we say "fairy," we're actually talking about a mythical, imaginary, supernatural creature. How it jumped to be known as an effeminate man, I don't know.

Nigger, Nigga, Niggah, N-word. Even if we were to resurrect some other archaic words, these are the exception. Can we PLEASE, finally bury *all* facets and references to these words as a classification for black people? All these words are derogatory, in any form. Even the word "niggard," which is British slang for a stingy person, a cheapskate, covetous, doesn't sound pleasant. If we want to refer to a black person, why not simply say "black" (which is "negro" or "negra" in Spanish; "noir" in French; "schwarz" in German; "kuro" in Japanese; "kaala" in Hindi; and "nyeusi" in Swahili; among many others).

Queer. Long before the word "queer" became associated with sexual orientation, it simply meant different, not fitting into any standard category, fluidity of personality. In fact, Associate Professor Timothy W. Jones of La Trobe University, writes, "Queer . . . entered the English language by the early 16th century, when it was primarily used to mean strange, odd, peculiar or eccentric." As the definition points out, "queer" doesn't mean homosexual. A heterosexual person can be queer (eccentric, odd, different, not fitting into what we call regular society).

Speed. Even *I* knew this wasn't originally a word for LSD. But I did think it meant driving fast. So imagine my surprise when I learned that it originally meant prosperity and success.

Weed. Another surprising word. Not only was it not originally a slang for marijuana, it also didn't mean a wild growing grass. Weed originally meant a garment or outfit worn during mourning.

Weird. This word comes from the Old English noun wyrd, which essentially means "fate." It is said to mean that someone has the ability to control their own destiny. (Oxford Language Dictionary and Miriam-Webster Dictionary on the www.)

Wood. Head out of the gutter, folks. ☺ To those who may be thinking it, this is *not* a sexual reference. Wood originally meant mad, insane or wild.

Of Course I'm Irish

It rained on and off all day, March 17, 1990. The day began with grey clouds hanging low in the early morning sky. Then shortly after 9:30, the sun peeped through and scattered the clouds into tiny, light gray pillows that floated aimlessly across the sky. "Ahh, this day is gonna turn out great after all," I said, as I pulled back the living room curtains.

Our family's house stood on a small hill at the intersection of Roosevelt and Giles Street. On the opposite corner of the intersection, diagonal from ours, stood a beautiful rose-colored house, the most picturesque one on the block.

I stood in the window for a few minutes watching Mrs. May mow her lawn. Nearly 78 years old, she worked at the same pace as a woman half her age. She'd been that way ever since I'd known her, working at something, doing this and that. But most of her attention went to her yard, which was the trademark of the neighborhood. No stranger in town ever had trouble finding her house. People just directed them to the house, trimmed in burgundy, with the immaculately tailored lawn. "You can't miss it," they'd say. "Just look for the hedges carved in the shape of a dog or a basket, or the initials 'DH'" (in honor of her late husband).

As I watched Mrs. May, I saw something that I hadn't noticed during the entire ten minutes I stood in in the window watching her. It struck me that she was wearing a kelly green jumpsuit. Then I remembered, "Oh. I forgot that today is St. Patrick's Day."

That stirred something inside me, for I am an old sentimental fool at heart. (Yes, I cry at weddings, stand in pride when I hear the National Anthem, and melt when watching rom-coms.) But something about this scenario also gave me pause. Something I'd never thought about before. Here was this dark-skinned Black woman, wearing in a green jumpsuit, in a rural Southern town, celebrating an Irish holiday.

Maybe it was because I had just read Alice Walker's *You Can't Keep a Good Woman Down*, or maybe it was my recent "awokeness," thinking about my enslaved great-grandmother, or my neighbors who struggled to make ends meet, or perhaps it was "just because." Whatever the reason, it suddenly struck me that most African-Americans celebrate all things American but not all of America celebrates us. Neither are all things American ours to celebrate.

My mind drifted back to the early seventies, when I wore green to work *every* St. Patrick's Day. Some of my office colleagues (95% of them were white at the time) jokingly said, "I didn't know you were Irish, Evelyn." Back then, I never thought anything of it, so I'd grin slyly, and quip, "Sure I am. On my daddy's side through my uncle Kunte O'Leary."

I look back on those days and thank God I don't have to play those games anymore. Oddly, though, now that I don't have to play those games anymore and can speak my mind, for some reason I don't want to. Don't get me wrong. I realize injustice and hatred still rage, but for some reason I don't feel the need to fight people on every little issue. Yes, I see crooked politicians spouting vile accusations. I see broken promises and broken dreams. I see society getting worse day by day. But somehow I've come to realize that fighting and raging don't necessarily create change. I've come to realize that every time you raise your voice in anger, the attention that you get is usually negative. When you fight others, it causes others to fight back, or worse yet, they simply ignore you. Either way, your "fight" runs the risk of going for naught. I've come to realize that to subdue the loud, roaring enemy, the ultimate war must be done with quiet virtue.

What is "quiet virtue"? Quiet virtue is being still in the face of chaos and confusion. Quiet virtue is holding your peace while at the same time standing tall against warmongers. Quiet virtue is exuding humility while maintaining dignity and showing courage in the face of danger. Quiet virtue is what I believe Dr. Martin Luther King, Rosa Parks, the Manhattan Silent Protesters of 1917, the A&T Four, and many others understood and demonstrated. They realized that victory over our enemies was rooted in non-violence. Martin Luther King, of course, relied on the Bible for much of his inspiration, and believe it or not, the answer to winning the great war has always been in the Bible. (But the fruit of the Spirit is love, joy, peace, forbearance, kindness, goodness, faithfulness, gentleness, and self-control. Against such things there is no law. (Galatians 5:22-23))

Some may disagree with me, and that's okay. Discourse is good. In the final analysis, we're all working for change.

Whether we believe in non-violent social change – such as was demonstrated by King and others, or

change by any means necessary, such as was used in a
speech by Malcolm Little (a.k.a., Malcolm X), or even
change in the form of peace and harmony such as was
aluded to when Rodney King said, "Can we all get
along?" – I hope we can all agree that change is
needed. We cannot give up the fight for change,
especially now. We cannot afford to stop believing, as
Sam Cooke said, "A change is gonna come."

PART V: PERSONAL OBSERVATIONS AND INTERCONNECTIVENESS

All around us are things of wonder and delight. Rainbows, water falls, mountains, blue skies, even cloudy days, are all beautiful parts of Nature. Like a grand symphony, Nature interlocks and intertwines everything together so that they all work in harmony with each other. Isn't that wonderful?

Birds, Nature's Cheerleaders

Hands down, song birds have got to be the happiest, most optimistic creatures alive. They start chirping early in the morning, even before the rooster crows. They sing all through the day, and when evening comes, they're the last "voices" you hear before the crickets start to sing.

Birds sing in the rain. Their songs signify that fair weather is coming. During a storm, though, birds sit quietly and wait for the storm to pass. What a powerful image!

Birds, I think, have the right philosophy about life. I wonder how much better we'd feel if we acted more like birds. What if, at the beginning of each day – long before the thought of the day's tasks filled our heads – we just broke out in song? What if we just whistled while we worked as Snow White did?* What if we let a smile be our umbrella?** Or maybe we could relieve some anxiety and fear if we would Whistle A Happy Tune.***

Yes, birds are remarkable singers, but birds can teach us so many other lessons about life. Check out Will Hall's list of things we can learn from birds.

1. Be confident. Birds rely on their wings to lift them up to new places and new adventures. Guillemots nest along cliff edge. When their juveniles become too large to stay at the nest site, these semi-flightless birds throw themselves into the icy waters below with complete confidence and instinct. The upshot: Don't let your nervousness be the reason you miss out on a leap of faith.

2. **Let your colours shine**. Birds of Paradise are masters of colour and performance are not afraid to be themselves and to let their eccentricities shine. Many are adorned in wonderfully colourful and exotic plumage and others create such stunning dances and flourishes that they would show up any professional dancer. Perhaps we could learn from the birds of paradise to let our true colours shine through.

3. **Show up early and often.** The early bird catches the worm- an old adage which certainly has its roots in truth. Early birds are more likely to survive by finding more food. Although getting up early for us might be a lot less crucial, creating and practicing good habits can lead to a healthier and happier life; so find something worth getting up early for and commit to it.

4. **Go with the seasons.** Some birds are seasonal of course, heading south in the winter in search of warmer climates or heading north on the hunt for a place to breed. Sometimes the pull of the seasons is all that's needed to nudge us along our path.

5. **Be a good parent**. Many birds will go to any lengths to protect their young, even putting themselves into danger to secure a safer life for their babies. Take the Killdeer for example. These brave little birds will mob and feign injury to distract a predator. They will throw themselves onto the ground flapping and flailing to draw the predator closer. Surely there is no greater indication of a parent's love?

6. **Flock together.** What better example of flocking is there than Starling murmuration. Some think that these enormous groups come together to evade predators, meet prospective mates, or to exchange information. However, the most popular belief is that they do it to strengthen bonds, find friends and make new ones. This

is certainly something we too could practice; find
comfort in our friends and family and keep those bonds
strong throughout our life.

7. Spread your wings. Eventually, no matter how
comfy and cozy the nest might be, there is something
which calls to young fledglings to take the leap. The
Californian Condor, for example, can spend up to six
months in its nest before finally taking flight. Despite
being one of the United State's largest birds, it is still a
little nervous to head out into the world too soon. Just
as condors need to take flight eventually, as humans we
also have to be brave, spread our wings, and find our
own space to explore and thrive.

8. Return home. One of the big life lessons we can
learn from nature is the tendency to return home
eventually. There is something deep within the natural
world which calls individuals to return home at the
right time. The juvenile, Northern Gannet, for example,
may not return home after the first year. However,
something calls to the youngsters when it's time for
them to make the journey back to where they were
born. Although our birth place may not always be the
"right" place for us, we need to be able to recognise
and respond to the call of home, if and when it comes.

9. Be always cheerful. Have you ever sat at a window
on a cold and wet day and watched the thrushes
singing? Or observed a pair of pigeons cooing over one
another amidst the drizzle? Have you ever seen the
evident joy from a blackbird as she bathes in a muddy
puddle? Or seen a woodpecker pulling at a worm on a
frosty day? It is possibly the greatest life lesson to be
cheerful no matter the weather. When the rain clouds
gather and storms come into our lives, let's keep
positive and sing in the rain.

The conclusion, says Hall, is that at first glance the
lives of birds are simple and carefree but as we can see,

they are anything but that. They lead challenging existences fraught with danger and yet they move forward and remain a constant source of joy for everyone. We can learn a great deal from nature and from simply watching birds. This mindful practice is an essential part of our growth. Finding solace in the simple things and learning from the world around us.

Wow! Lessons from birds. Who knew?

*Walt Disney Production, *Snow White and the Seven Dwarfs*. Song written by songwriter Larry Morey

**Credit Sammy Fain for the music.

***Richard Rodgers and Oscar Hammerstein, II, from *The King and I.*

Césped, Eushb, Gras, Herbe, Ruoho, Grass

Would you have bothered to read this section if I had simply titled it "Grass?" I doubt it. But since you're here, hang out with me for a little while. You may be as surprised as I was to learn so many fascinating facts about this little plant that so many people tend to discount.

This commentary about grass all began one Sunday morning when I was sitting in my car, relaxing before walking across the street to church. The glare of the early morning sun forced me to protract my visor, and as I did so, I noticed a trail of grass pushing up through the asphalt in the parking lot. "Hmmmm," I thought. "That's incredible. To think that those tiny little shoots somehow found their way through a seemingly impenetrable surface." I jotted down a note to remind myself to research "grass" when I got home. Even as I wrote, I scolded myself for obsessing over something so insignificant, so mundane. "Evelyn, you're about the weirdest person in the world," I thought as I continued writing. "Who else even notices – let alone perseverates – about something of so little importance?"

To some people grass is indeed unimportant. Many people see it as bothersome, a nuisance. To them, grass is the enemy, so they chop it, spray it, weed it, all in an effort to rid their territory of the envasive green shoots.

For others, grass is a welcome sight. They treasure its coverage, laud its lushness, marvel at its hue, and with joy, accept its invitation to lie in it. I happen to be somewhere in the middle. On the *one* hand, I don't want grass in my flowers, my garden, shooting up between the branches of my shrubbery, or growing taller than my sidewalk. On the other hand, there's nothing more beautiful than a lush, green lawn, or field full of sod. And what's a golf course without a smooth putting green?

After church service, still in the grips of curiosity (fueled by my OCD), I rushed home, went immediately to my computer, and typed the word "grass" in the search prompt. I fully expected to find absolutely nothing but a definition. Not so. I was overwhelmingly surprised to find so many of articles about this lowly little, ubiquitous plant.

Not only was there a myriad of grass facts, but lo and behold (yes, a "lo" *and* a "behold"), I was astonished to learn that there were other outside-the-box thinkers like me.

Much of what I write below comes from Geoff Horswood,* who was inspired by Kneika Robbins' post.** While reading their grass facts, I was immediately struck by how closely grass mimics human behavior and what we could learn from it. As I read, I wrote a few comments below their facts. (Since you've read this far, why stop now? Aren't you the least bit curious too?)

1. Grass is small and grows from the bottom up.
    (Hmmm. Is this like saying that grass is humble, not puffed up, and is willing to start small and work its way up, the same as we do on jobs and in life?)
2. Grass was meant to be grazed, that is, to help others. Grass is used as fodder for cattle, deer and all sorts of other animals. (To be grazed, to me, means that

we give of ourselves. In addition to that, when grass is used to feed animals, we in turn use these animals for food. So grass sustains us.)

3. Grass grows where it seems impossible to grow. You can strip away all the topsoil, lay concrete or asphalt over it, and in due time, grass will find a way to poke its little head out. Grass grows in sidewalks, on the side of mountains, in gutters, and, given time, even in cracks in window sills. (This, perhaps, may lead us to act in impossible situations or speak life into someone's spirit. One good word of encouragement might be the catalyst that changes a person's life.)

4. Grass isn't a loner. It doesn't usually grow by itself. (Like grass, we need each other. We're stronger together.)

Aside from these interesting facts from Mr. Horswood, I found other grass facts on various websites.

*   Grass is resilient. Chop it down, it comes back. Spray it with weed killer, it lies dormant for a while, then comes back. Dig it up, it throws out little gametes that germinate elsewhere. (Like grass, what if we didn't give up in the face of adversity?)

*   Grass protects the soil. It stops erosion. (What if we looked out for others more, protected our loved ones and stopped the erosion of the family circle and our communities?)

*   Some grasses (wheatgrass, for example) is often used as a source of nutrients. It contains vitamin A, vitamin C, vitamin E, iron, calcium, magnesium, and amino acids. Other types of grasses can be used as medicine for treatment as anti-emetic, intestinal parasites, indigestion, profuse menstruation, colds and bruises. (Hmmm. Is that why, as a child, I sometimes saw

our dogs eat grass? What did they know that we didn't? Humph. And we think we're the smart ones.)

- **Grass can be used as fuel.** (Put simply, dried grass burns, and rolled tightly together, it burns slower, creating a torch.)

- **Grass is a good insulating tool.** (What? You never saw people who live off the grid, stuff a mixture of grass and mud between the cracks in their log cabins?)

- **Grass can be used to make building materials.** (Now I know you know this one is possible. Remember the children of Israel? The Egyptians? How the Egyptians forced Israel to make bricks with clay and straw (dried grass)?

- **Grass can be used to make furniture.** (This last one is a little odd even to me, but I'm throwing it in here anyway. Admittedly, I didn't watch the videos on the www because they kept buffering, so when you get a chance look up "furniture from grass." There were several DIY videos on the subject.)

Grass facts from a *May 2014 article (public www posting on WordPress.com (site deleted by the authors)), citing Kneika Robbins' post **Serious Thoughts*). Other facts found on www.Google.com.

From The Small Grows The Great

Many people go about their daily lives never noticing the minute wonders of the world around them. A world that may seem vast and huge to some, in essence, is a finely woven tapestry of art, behaviors, emotions, and interconnections with everything and everybody.

It's easy to see a trail of ants as "just ants," but if you look closer, you'll see a whole city, communicating, living and working together in harmony for the good of all. Oh, what giants those tiny creatures are!

Small things matter. They are the building blocks on which larger things stand and benefit. In the grand scheme of things, something as small as phytoplankton and algae end up supporting mankind. As I understand it, phytoplankton and algae form the base elements of aquatic food chains. They are eaten by primary consumers, which in turn are eaten by secondary consumers which are eaten by tertiary consumers (animals that eat other animals, e.g., humans, who are both carnivorous and herbivorous).

A quote, credited to Benjamin Franklin, goes something like this: "For want of a nail the shoe was lost. For want of a shoe, the horse was lost. For want of a horse, the rider was lost. For want of a rider, the battle was lost. For want of the battle, the kingdom was lost."

What if we applied that analogy to the jobs that some people think are *in*significant? Looking at it from the standpoint of my "phytoplanktonian theory," that job may be the very thing that holds the company together. Imagine if Ben Franklin's quote read something like this: Because someone thought a few drops of water on the floor didn't matter, someone slipped in it. Because someone slipped in it, he/she was injured. Because he/she was injured, the company was sued. Because the company was sued, it went bankrupt. Because the company went bankrupt, two hundred employees lost their jobs.

Here's another one. What if the doctor wrote your prescription for 10 mcg (micrograms) and the pharmacy filled it for mg (milligrams, a much higher dose)?

And yet another. Do you know why banks used to insist that you draw a long line after you spelled out the amount? It's to keep people from adding extra words. The numbers in the little box are very easy to change, but without the line, "Thirty-five dollars" could easily become "Thirty-five hundred dollars." Thanks to a dear friend who taught me to jam everything together (e.g., "Thirty-five & 00/100"), I avoided bank account thieves.

A famous Scripture reads, in part, "Look also at ships: although they are so large and are driven by fierce winds, they are turned by a very small rudder wherever the pilot desires ...." Another reads, "See how great a forest fire is started by a little spark!" (James 3:4-5, paraphrased)

Small things are so important that they can make great changes in our lives, our nation, our world. Have you ever thought about just how far a little bit of kindness and love go? Just like sunshine dissipates clouds, and little smiles turn away frowns, so do kind words repel wrath, joy erases sorrow, positivity changes negativity, and above all, *love* trumps hate. To add to the good part about love is that it only takes a small amount, like a tiny mustard seed growing into a great bush.

The upshot of all of this is that we should never underestimate ourselves or think that we are small and insignificant. Even though humans may be a small speck in this vast universe of ours, each one of us matters and we have a lot to offer to each other. We all co-exist to make the world what it is. In the same way that an atom needs protons, neutrons and electrons to be complete, all of us need each other for the greater good. WE are the protons, neutrons, and electrons – the catalysts – from which greater things grow.

PART VI: NOSTALGIA, SIMPLER TIMES

If time travel ever really became a possibility, I'd
be the first to jump in line . . . after it had been well
tested, of course. My first stop? 1957-1961. Those were
my elementary school years, my age of innocense.
(Middle school hadn't been invented yet.) Nowadays,
those memories dart in and out of my mind like a flash
on a camera. When I catch myself daydreaming about
all the wonderful days of my youth, I remind myself
that even though I can't bring those days back, I still
can relish in a few stolen moments.

Old Sayings

I thought this section might be good for some people to learn (and for others to recall) some of the things parents used to tell us when we were young. We passed many of them on to our children, hoping that they, in turn, would pass them on to theirs. Here are just a few:

Old Saying	Translation/Meaning
It's a poor frog that won't praise its own pond.	A person ought to be proud enough of his/her own (family, town, country, etc.) to stand up for it, or even boast a little.
Not a telephone but a hellaphone.	People use telephones to gossip, spread lies, sow dissent, etc., all the things that create trouble.
Every tub has to stand on its own bottom.	You need to be responsible for yourself and what you do.
You made your bed hard now lie in it.	Accept the consequences of your bad choices.

Two can keep a secret if one is dead.	The best way to make sure a secret doesn't get out is to keep it to yourself.
Haste makes waste.	Rushing causes you to make mistakes.
A stitch in time saves nine.	Stopping small trouble when it happens keeps it from turning into something bigger.
Poor planning on your part doesn't mean an emergency on my part.	I'm not rushing to do something just because you didn't prepare.
A chain is only as strong as its weakest link.	Even the strongest system, organization, group, structure, plan, etc., will fall apart where the weakest point is.
A bird in hand is worth two in the bush.	What you have now is better than what is promised.
Many hands make light work.	Sharing the workload makes it easier on everyone.
Don't throw the baby out with the bathwater.	If you're not careful, you can lose something good or valuable while trying to get rid of something unwanted.

People who live in glass houses shouldn't throw stones.	Remember your own faults before you criticize others.
The pot can't call the kettle black.	Don't point a finger at someone else's faults when you have the same, or similar, ones.
Don't look a gift horse in the mouth.	Be grateful. Don't find fault with a gift that has been given to you.
Don't count your chickens before they hatch.	Don't make plans, or depend on something before you have the means by which to complete it.
You can't teach an old dog new tricks.	Teaching older people new things is challenging.
You've got a good head on your shoulders.	You are very intelligent.
The early bird catches the worm.	You will have an advantage if you act immediately, or act before other people do.

Birds of a feather flock together.	People who are alike, or who like the same things, hang around each other. Elders used this phrase to show us we shouldn't hang around the "bad" crowd, i.e., if people saw us with the wrong crowd, they would assume we were doing the same thing.
The tree that constantly leans never stands straight. (Evelyn, 2024)	If you always depend on someone else for everything, you'll never learn to be independent.

Milk and Honey in Heaven

When I was a little girl, my grandmother said, "When we get to Heaven, we'll feast on milk and honey." She seemed so overjoyed at the idea that she beamed with delight every time she said it. To her, eating milk and honey in Heaven represented the culmination of a life well lived, the high point of becoming an Angel, or at least being able to frolic around with them.

The thing that was euphoric to my grandmother represented abject horror to me. You see, at the time, I didn't like honey. Even worse, the very thought of mixing it with milk turned my stomach. Besides that, I wondered what type of honey the Angels would use. Clover honey? Wildflower honey? Would it be organic? Pasteurized? Raw? And what kind of milk would they mix the honey in? Whole milk? Evaporated? Half-n-half? I certainly hoped it wouldn't be skim milk. Can you even classify that as milk? And would the milk be warm? I hoped not. I hated warm milk more than anything.

The fear of not being able to go to Heaven just because of a little thing like a glass of honey-sweetened milk, prompted me to try to get used to it. I'd seen on TV how everyone raved about how warm milk soothed anxiety and helped you sleep, so I tried it. After heating a cupful, I added enough honey to sweeten it, then took a cautious sip. Yuck! Just as I thought. It tasted awful! "Maybe I'll try mixing it with cold milk," I reasoned. "I love ice cold milk." Admittedly, it wasn't as bad as warm milk but still not palatable enough for me to live off of in Heaven. That's when a horrifying thought engulfed me. Even if I was fortunate to make it to Heaven, I'd starve to death in a matter of weeks. What a disaster.

You may have picked up the phrase, "Even if I was fortunate enough to make it to Heaven . . .." Well, the reason for that phrase is this: Aside from the milk and honey dilemma, I always knew I'd never get to see Heaven because I just *wasn't good* enough. I had a temper, was moody and sullen, and just plain didn't like people. So in my young mind, even if I could get used to milk and honey, I was still doomed.

Thank God for this thing called maturity. As I matured and learned more about God and the Bible, I discovered two most important things: First – and most importantly, *above all others* – getting into Heaven doesn't depend on how good you are. Whew! What a relief. Second, the milk-and-honey concept was a metaphor (a concept that I hadn't yet learned at my young age). It came from God's promise to the Israelites after their exodus from Egypt. God promised them a land "flowing with milk and honey." (Exodus 3:8; Numbers 14:8, and others).

Now that I'm older and wiser (supposedly), my aged self looks back at my younger self and laughs. It's funny how a child's mind misconstrues just about everything and cooks up the most outlandish fantasies. To a young child, everything that the mind *thinks* is real, is *very* real to them. Thank God for longevity. God allowed me to live long enough to outgrow so many of my childish illusions. (When I was a child . . . . 1 Cor. 13:11)

Fellow Dinosaurs Unite!

When I say to people "I'm a dinosaur," they chuckle politely and look at me with confusion and curiosity. What makes me a dinosaur? To me, it's my antiquated views in these modern times, coupled with what some might call outdated beliefs and values. Even the way I speak, how I think, and my approach to problem-solving make me seem like a lumbering behemoth, clashing with the neo/futuristic ideas and systems of today. These systems are sometimes as unfamiliar to me as the changing world was to dinosaurs of 65,000,000 years ago.

Think about it, though. Is being a dinosaur so bad? Don't we need modern-day dinosaurs? So, even if I'm "outdated," I don't believe I'm alone. I believe there are thousands of other dinosaurs out there just like me. So fellow dinosaurs unite with me . . .

- if you believe that respect should be given before it's received;
- if you believe being respectful garners respect;
- if you believe that law and order dispel chaos;
- if you are tired of hearing politicians say they are "fighting for everyone," but they never ask your opinion;
- if you think some of the old '50s and '60s ways were better;
- if you think gas is too high and males' pants are too low;

- if you think females wear too much make-up and too little clothing;
- if you think children are raising their parents, not the other way around;
- if you think you shouldn't have to press "1" for English in an English-speaking country;
- if you believe that prayer (and even Bible verses, as well) should be put back in schools;
- if you think that we shouldn't strip *all* police of their authority because of a few bad ones;
- if you think police shouldn't have to say, "Do me a favor..." or "Do you mind if I search you?";
- if you believe that some criminals did commit the crimes of which they are accused;
- if you believe that the system is set up so that it's not about having a criminal answer for the crime but more about who can afford the best lawyer;
- if you believe some lawyers are going to hell for getting criminals off when they know they're guilty, and some are going there for putting people in jail when they know they're innocent;
- if you believe the phrase "honest politician" is an oxymoron.

National Over Seventy Anthem

Oh, say can you see, by the dawn's early light?
No, I can't see a thing,
*   at least not without my glasses.*
They're around somewhere,
*   'cause I had them last night.*
I laid them on the table,
*   right next to my knitting basket.*

The TV was playing,
*   and I was talking on the phone,*
Until I realized no one was there,
*   'cause all I heard was a dial tone.*
Then I took out my teeth and put them inside a cup
So I could find them the next day when I woke up.

Oh say does that noise
*   sound like a loud squeaky gate?*
I really don't know 'cause I also lost my hearing aid.

**

Oh the joy of waking up and beginning a new day!
I think I'll go walking on the trail along the river.
There are healing herbs on that trail,
*   or so people say.*
I'd better get going before my knees get any stiffer.

Let me check all the things that think I will need.
Got some fruit, water, and a few sunflower seeds.
Checking my supplies as I head for the door

Oh wait.
    Did I already do that before?

Oh say does this banner of pride
    and courage yet wave.
Old age ain't for sissies; it's only for the brave!

Tess

Before she passed away in 2023, my dear friend, Tess (not her real name) and I shared many leisurely days, whiling away the hours, people-watching and just being silly. Tess and I were members of a seven-person travel/social group of seniors. Members of the group were spread across three counties, but Tess and I lived in the same town, so we'd get together a couple of times a week without the other members. Our favorite pastime was watching pedestrians and street traffic from the edge of some store's parking lot. Don't ask me why we never commandeered a park bench somewhere or sat on the edge of a lake. Who knows? We were content to just pull up in our separate cars, shut off the engines, and ponder "the ways of the world."

On any given day, Tess would call me and say, "Hey, I'm tired of messin' with these figures. Let's go grab a snowball and drive over to [so-and-so] street." Then we'd both drop whatever we were doing and head to the rendevous point. There we'd sit in the privacy of our cars, roll down the windows and talk through the opening. (Again, why one of us didn't jump into the other's car, I don't know.) Like two old biddies sitting on the front porch, rocking back and forth, we laughed at every little crazy thing that crossed our minds. Sometimes we even laughed at ourselves over how silly we must look to others. But that was Tess and me.

Tess and I shared the same satirical sense of humor, and the one thing we enjoyed most was witty TV commercials. Our favorites were the Geico® camel,

Progressive's® Dr. Rick, the eTrade® baby, and Allstate's® "Mayhem." Actually, we appreciated *any* company's inventive commercials. If it was funny and witty, we watched it with delight, but the ones mentioned stood out above the rest. At times, it seemed like we watched TV more for the commercials than for the program, and we critiqued them as if we were getting paid to do so.

Commercials. Sports. Traveling. Food. Our college days. Society. No subject was off limits. One day, while gabbering on about everything from moon landings to places we wanted to see, Tess suddenly blurted out, "Will somebody please tell these parents to stop putting apostrophes in their children's names to make them look fancy? The poor children gonna grow up not knowing how to pronounce their own name when they see it." Startled, I said, "Well, you just threw that one right in there, didn't you, Tess. I thought we were talking about adobe houses and visiting the vortex in Sedona. Give me a warning next time you switch subjects in your head." Then we'd both fall out laughing. That was the beauty of our friendship. Neither of us needed to explain the joke. We just knew.

Late one evening, the phone rang. It was Tess. "Hey, remember when we were talking about apostrophes in kids' names?"

"Yeah," I answered, curiously, getting myself ready for more Tess comedy. "Well, here's what I was thinking. Not only apostrophes, but what about these three- and four-syllable names? What's wrong with the good old regular names like John and James?" She paused, and before I could answer, she added, "But if

they want some three and four-syllable names, why not
Ni-cho-las or Tim-o-thy or even Bar-tho-lo-mew?" she
said, sounding out each syllable. "Bartholomew is a
four-syllable name." Then we laughed 'til our sides
ached. But before we could recover, she added, "I think
I'll name my next baby L'Tanyashekah, or
LaRa'Sheed'a. That's apostrophes *and* four syllables."
We howled at *that* joke because we were both in our
late sixties, well past child-bearing age.

Sometimes, when I reminisce, I remember one of
Tess's favorite lines: "That women must not have any
real friends." "Why?" I'd ask, already knowing her
answer. "Because, if she had any real friends, they
wouldn't have let her leave the house looking like
that." The "that" could be anything from a woman
trying to fit a size 28 body into a size 18 pair of pants,
to someone wearing a wig dyed bright orange, lime
green, or turquoise blue. "God didn't make us be born
with bright green hair, so how can that look natural?"

There were times when Tess and I laughed at each
other over our own shortcomings. You see, Tess was a
mathematician and I'm a wordsmith. *She* could do
complex equations in her head but stumbled when it
came to spelling words above two syllables without
writing them down, syllable-by-syllable. On the other
hand, *I* could spell almost anything and write in
compound/complex sentences, but couldn't figure out
some math problems, even *with* a calculator. So, here's
the irony: If we wanted to slip away from a gathering
where small children were around, I might whisper to
her, "Hey. Let's make a run to F-r-a-n-c-o-s and get
dessert." But the deer-in-headlights look on her face

told me that she didn't have a clue about what I said. "Oh," I continued. "I need to speak your language. I said, let's make a run to six-eighteen-one . . .."

That may have been a "one up" for me, but her payback came when she'd see me struggling with math. It could be something as simple as trying to calculate time and distance on a trip, or adjusting measurements in a recipe. After watching me squirm, just when I was near tears, she'd simply grin and give me the answer. Frustrated, I'd say, "Well, I was close," to which she would repeat part of an old Frank Robinson quote, "Close only counts in horseshoes and hand grenades."

Tess and I were like sisters, and now that she's gone, I feel like a part of me is gone too. I miss our commercial commentaries, our sports watching sessions, and mostly, the trips that we took with our traveling group. Periodically, I touch bases with our group, and many others with whom Tess was acquainted. We all feel the same way. Tess was a very special person who touched many hearts. She had a way of dealing with people that was soothing. Even the hottest head was no match for Tess's calm demeanor. Everyone who knew her said she taught them so much about themselves, and about life. Rest in peace, Tess. We all miss you.

PART VII: THE END CYCLES BACK TO THE BEGINNING

Do you ever think about how life comes full circle? How the end of one experience leads to the beginning of another? How one relevation or epiphany opens the door to another?

Whether it's roads of physical travel, spiritual roads of faith, or metaphysical roads of self-awareness, when it's all said and done – when we've lived, learned, and laughed – we can appreciate our wonderful, rich life. It's at that stage that we realize that life is not over. It's just beginning.

Third "I" Blind

This is not a discourse about Third Eye Blind, the American rock band formed in San Francisco, California, in 1993, although I do like the theme of some of their songs, especially those that call attention to needless suicide because of the pressures of bullying and hatred. I also like the ones that depict the dream of being in a better place and reaching for a better way of life.

So if not about the rock band, then what is this segment about? For starters, first look at what the "third eye" is. The "third eye" (also called the mind's eye or inner eye), is associated with religious visions, clairvoyance and people's ability to observe chakras (main energy points in the body) and auras (the "energy" that a person projects). The third eye represents mystical intuition and insight (an inner vision and enlightenment beyond what the physical eyes can see). On statues, in paintings and other artwork, the third eye is depicted as a single eye in the center of the forehead. When the chakras are not functioning to their fullest, the third eye is said to be clouded, or sometimes, blind.

By now, I hope you've noticed that I titled this writing, Third *I* Blind. Akin to what the third *eye* represents in spirituality and mysticism, the third *I*, to me, is how we see ourselves. It's how we think we fit into society. It's how and where we project ourselves to be in the vast sea of other humans. Sigmund Freud might call it "ego" – or in some cases – "super ego." But I think it goes much deeper than the egos.

For some, their third *I* is secure. Some might even say it's overly dominant. They *know* what they want. They *do* what they want. They *go* where they want to go. They visualize how they want their lives to be, then press on and move forward toward that vision . . . sometimes without regard to others. Their third *I* is anything but blind.

For others, however, their third *I* might be blocked, clouded, even blinded, if you will. The third-*I*-blind people, might feel rejected or insecure. They may be filled with a sense of inadequacy and self-doubt. As a result, they may feel that their contributions (or even themselves) are not worthwhile. Third *I* blind people tend to allow others to step ahead of them, not out of courtesy, but out of a sense of obligation because they don't think they measure up.

But here's the thing: No matter what third *I* blind people may think of themselves, we all know that third I blind people are very much needed. They are valuable. So to all who may think you're third *I* blind, let me offer you this encouragement: You have worth in this world. No matter what someone says about you, or how they try to tear you down, you are somebody! *You* are the true team players because you serve from the heart. You don't look for accolades, awards or pats on the back. Your contribution to the world is significant. You matter so much that the world could not exist without you. Let me illustrate just how important you are.

Do you remember Dr. Seuss's, *Horton Hears a Who*? The town of Whoville, which was on the verge of annihilation, was not saved because of Horton. It also wasn't saved because of Morton, the mouse, and *certainly* wasn't saved by the sour kangaroo. No. The town of Whoville was saved by the *smallest* word ("Yopp!"), uttered by the *smallest* child, with the *smallest* voice in the McDodd family.

So wake up and stand up, third *I* blind people. Wipe the clouds from your *I*. Assert yourself. Be bold and courageous. We need your wisdom, your friendship and leadership. We need your contributions to society. We need your energy, your drive, your motivation. We need your love, your caring. Without you, our little dust speck of a world would crumble. We need your "Yopp!"

The Fourth Quarter

My sister-in-law, Janice, recently celebrated her seventy-fifth birthday. It was a grand event, held outside at a country club, with Southern catered food. We laughed, played games (for which she gave presents to us when we won), and had mega fun. The DJ was fantastic! Not only did he play upbeat music throughout the party, but he also provided specially selected songs for a game that Janice had created, that she called "Name-That-Artist."

A few days after the party, Janice called me, just to chat, as we occasionally did, and I congratulated her on a wonderfully entertaining party. During our conversation, she said that one of her friends had remarked, "You know you're in the fourth quarter of life, don't you?" I was so appalled that anyone would say such a thing that I started fussing right away. Well, Janice must have sensed that I was about to get my knickers in a knot, so she calmed me down. "Wait. Wait." She said. "It wasn't like you think. It was actually positive, insightful, and encouraging. Just listen."

After a few cautious seconds, Janice continued. "What she meant was this: When we reach our 70s, it's time for us to stop holding back on life. It's time to live a little (or a lot) and have some fun." She went on, "We spend all our lives putting other things ahead of ourselves . . . our jobs, our families, scrimping and saving to secure a comfortable future. At this stage of our lives, it's time to stop withholding our enjoyment of life and have some fun. I thought what my friend said was a beautiful analogy about life." After that she asked, "By the way, what sport has four quarters? Is it football or basketball?"

"It's basketball," I chuckled. Then, we had a fantastic, enlightening, conversation about how life is analogeous to a game of basketball.

FIRST QUARTER (the early years). The game has just begun. You're getting a feel of the court, your surroundings, and the other players. You're also learning what things the "referees" will and will not allow. You have excellent coaches, that have taught you know things about good sportsmanship, respect, fairness, etc. You know that your team members are your allies, so you've learned to play as a team. Because you're on a winning team, the game is relatively easy for you and the team begins to rack up points (valuable investments of money, knowledge, life lessons, etc., for the future).

SECOND QUARTER (the middle years; nesting, building for the future). Your team is way ahead, and things look great for you. No problems in sight. You're still having fun but you notice that some players on the other team are beginning to get frustrated. You sense that they're jealous of your success, but you think to yourself, "I can't help it if my coaches prepared me well," but you don't say anything to offend or embarrass them. You just keep playing.

Midway through the second quarter, you start to tire a little. "Where's this coming from?" you ask yourself. "When I started out, I was fresh, ready to play, full of energy. Now I'm feeling like I want to rest every time I go up and down the court." Something else, too. Now, more than ever, you begin to feel the bumps and shoves from the players on the other team. Plus, you notice that they are not playing fairly. They push you around, even knock you down sometimes, and the refs don't even call a foul on them. You're frustrated, but your coaches say, "Just settle down. Keep playing. You're strong. You've been preparing for this all your life. You can do it. Just focus."

HALFTIME (time to evaluate your progress thus far and plan for the rest of the "game"). Your coaches help you take this opportunity to evaluate everything so far. Sure, there were a few bumps and bruises in the first two quarters, but you remembered all the fundamentals of the game that you'd been taught. It's time to put aside all the frustrations of the first two quarters and get back in the game. You and your coaches have worked out a strong plan for the last two quarters. All you have to do is execute. Your coaches remind you that you are surrounded by a strong team, people who will be there for you. They won't let you down. If you pass the ball, they will catch it. If you commit a foul, they will take up the slack. And, ohhh, if you miss a free throw, one of them will be sure to get your rebound!

THIRD QUARTER (the maturing years; ready, set, go; all is well). You start out strong again. Everything looks rosey . . for a while. Oh, but what's this?! You get pushed in the back? Knocked down? Your ankle folds at an awkward angle and you fall to the floor in pain. The coach takes you out of the game and calls for the team doctor. You hope it's not broken because it would be a disaster for you to come out of the game at this point. You have so much more time to play.

They spray your ankle with an anti-inflamatory medicine, wrap it and pack it in ice. While sitting on the bench, anxious, waiting, you think to yourself, "I've got to fight through this pain. I can't give up now."

Soon the team doctor comes over to recheck your ankle. He asks you to move it around. It hurts a little but you don't dare tell him. He scratches his head and asks you to move it again. Then, to your surprise, he says you can go back in the game but you'll need to be very careful because that ankle injury is a sign that there could be worse things to come.

FOURTH QUARTER (time to relax and enjoy the rest of the game). This is the most crucial part of the game. You've taken the lumps and bruises. You've been a team player. You've supported everyone else. You've stuck by your teammates and followed your coaches' instructions. Throughout the game the opposing team put up a lot of shots. They even pulled ahead a couple of times, but didn't stay there for long. Your team is ahead now, and you realize that what you do in these last few minutes of this last quarter determines how you leave the court. Your coaches remind you that you're on a winning team. You've played well. You've overcome obstacles. You've accomplished so much. There won't be a need for a last-second miracle shot to win the game. All you have to do is just relax and finish the last few minutes.

****

Janice enthusiastically finished her story and added some insightful words of her own: "The fourth quarter is the time you start to live for yourself, to enjoy life. It's after you've lived through all the uncertain years of trying to figure out who you are and what you want to do. You've married, raised the kids, bought a house (or two, or more). You're satisfied that you've done your best. Now all you need to do is relax, have fun, and enjoy the rest of the 'game.'"

PART VIII: AN AUTOBIOGRAPHICAL LOOK AT WHAT LED TO WRITING *TRULY GROUNDED*

Why does the autobiographical background appear at the end, you ask? Well, after reading part of *Truly Grounded*, one of my editors said that the arrangement of stories or chapters in a book determine whether someone will keep reading it or put it down after the first few lines. She suggested that I rearrange some stories and delete others, and put them in a future work. However, my sense of control and obsessive-compulsive tendencies wouldn't let me ditch *any* of the stories. I had poured my heart and soul into this book and every time I write, it's with the notion that it's the last. When inspiration comes, I write until I've exhausted all the thoughts that come to mind, then I quit. That's why there is such a conglomeration of mixed-genres in this book. Yes, inspiration usually comes back but I don't know that at the time. So I put my heart and soul into everything I write, and to let go of any part of this book was like letting go of a part of me.

I did consider what my editor said, though, and compromised. Rather than putting the Background at the beginning where it might *not* have grabbed your attention, I put it here, at the end, after you had a chance to read all the other pieces. Another reason I wouldn't let go of the Background is because it tells the whole story of how I arrived at writing *Truly Grounded*. So, you can be the judge of whether I should have led with it or not. Either way, it's okay.

Background: How Did I Get Here?

So you want to know how I got to this point in my life, huh? Well, it all started when my dad, John Holt, married my mom, Annie Oldham. Just kiddin'. That's another story for a different book. I guess you really want to know how I evolved to this point in my writing experience, right? To answer that question, let me start with some questions of my own.

Who is a writer? Is a writer someone who is externally created (i.e., how others define you)? Is a writer internally created (how you define yourself)? Or is a writer Divinely created (who you are, absent any human thought or intervention)? These questions then lead to the question of what is writing? Is writing simply the ability to manipulate words in some sort of syntactical form? Or is writing the understanding of how to string sentences together in appealing and systematic ways? Maybe writing is all of the above. If so, then I've been a writer since sixth grade when I wrote poems and short stories in elementary school.

For me, writing is not what I do. It's who I am. However, I didn't know the *who* part – that is, I never thought of myself as being a writer – until 1988 when I met Amanda MacKay at the Festival for the Eno in Durham, North Carolina. That year, Festival organizers had decided to pair unknown/undiscovered writers like me with accomplished, published authors. I don't know how they got my name but I was honored to share the program with Ms. MacKay.

After my session, I stayed to listen to Ms. MacKay read from her book, *Death on the Eno*. Later, during a conversation with her, I confessed that I didn't understand why I had such an obsession with writing. I told her that I'd never tried to get anything published, but writing was like an insatiable addiction, an unquenchable fire.

She listened patiently, and with four, simple words, revealed my truth. "Writers can't *not* write," she said. Those words struck me as unfamiliar yet gratifying at the same time. I'd never thought of myself as a bona fide writer, let alone been called one before. Yet here was Amanda MacKay, an accomplished author by her own right, calling me a writer. Those four words changed my whole perspective about myself.

One would think that Ms. MacKay's validation would have catapulted me into a fabulous writing career, but it didn't. Being a professional writer takes time . . . lots of time, and time was what I didn't have. You see, I was working full-time, going to school full-time, and raising two children, one of whom was chronically ill. So writing professionally sat on the back burner like a slow simmering pot being stirred occasionally. The "stirring," for me, was assignments for my job and college classes.

Before I continue, let me digress for a minute to take you on another leg of my journey. Walk with me. It'll only take a minute or two. Maybe three or four. Five tops. Six maybe? Here we go.

I believe our paths in life are Divinely inspired. The roads we take and the careers we choose are actually orchestrated by God in order to fulfill a certain purpose. Although our paths may take several crooks and turns along the way – and sometimes we may not know where the road is taking us – we still end up exactly where we need to be at exactly the right time. Along each leg of our journey, we can gain valuable insights if we are tuned in and listening with our hearts.

That having been said, for me my heart had two loves. You already know about my love of writing, but I didn't tell you that I love teaching equally as well. Given the opportunity, I could teach all day and never get enough, which is why I believe both teaching and writing are cherished callings. I also believe that God led me down the path of teaching as my career profession in order to fulfill a certain purpose during that time in my life.

During my teaching career, people said I inspired them in so many ways, but the truth is, *they* inspired *me*. I learned so many valuable life lessons just from being in the presence of fellow educators and the students I taught. Among other things, being a teacher taught me how to accept people for who they are and to value *everyone*. It also taught me how to get along with others and not be so introverted and stoic. Through teaching, I learned to form lasting, meaningful bonds.

While in the workforce, I published two books. The first one, *Don't Mind If I Do: Classroom Warm-Up Exercises To Sharpen the Min*d, was published by a reputable, educational publisher. It was my first attempt at publishing but I had no strategic plan for how I would get it into the hands of schools across the nation. By the time I figured out some of the logistics, schools had moved into the world of digital learning and the age group for which the book was written, now got their gratification and motivation from bells, whistles, and other animated devices on their computer and smartphones. I still have one copy of that book as a lasting reminder of a time when I ventured out of my comfort zone and challenged myself.

My other book, *To My Brown Babies: A Great-Grandmother's Letter to African-American Girls and Their Friends*, was self-published. It felt good to see my work advertised on popular websites, but as anyone who has ever self-published knows, it is not for the faint of heart. It's also not for anyone lean in the pocketbook. That's because, in addition to *paying* someone to print your book, you must be your own agent, manager, editor and promoter. You have to take out ads, seek out writers' markets, and pay for venues to host readings. I didn't do any of that. One reason was lack of time, but if I'm being completely honest, it was mainly because I still struggled with Asociality and didn't like being in the public's eye. Besides that, by the time I finished *To My Brown Babies . . .*, I was in my sixties, with retirement just around the corner. So I figured I may as well wait until I retired to devote all my energy to writing and publishing. Naïvely, I thought that when I retired, I could finish all those other manuscripts I'd stored up over the years, submit them to a publisher, and Voila! My books would be on bookshelves all across the world! Boy was I wrong. Dead wrong. Not only was I wrong about easing into publishing, but worse yet, I was dead wrong about retirement. Let me digress, again, long enough to tell you about retirement.

Some of you may be thinking, "Wow! Retirement! You get to stay home all day, doing what you want, when you want. No more getting up at 5 AM, 'punching a clock.' No more dealing with 'stuff' all day and coming home tired and worn out, only to repeat the same process the next day." No more 9-to-5 routine. (Thanks for the song Dolly.) Y'all may be thinking that but not me. I *loved* my job and didn't want to leave it, but I'd be lying if I said I didn't view retirement with the same lustful thoughts as anyone else. So I have to admit, I was delighted when that day came. Delighted, that is, until I woke up on Day 1 of retirement.

It's funny how the anticipation of retirement is so exciting and exuberating, almost more than you can take. So, in the months, weeks, and days *leading up to* retirement, it felt like waiting for Christmas and the arrival of Santa Claus:

RETIREMENT'S COMING!! YAYYYY!!!
RETIREMENT'S COMING!! YAYYYY!!!
RETIREMENT'S COMING!! I CAN'T WAIT!!

Then retirement came. **Boom!**

Boom?

Boom is right. In the days and weeks *following* retirement, here's what it felt like to me:

RETIREMENT'S HERE!! YAYYYY!!
Retirement's here! Yayy!
Retirement's here? Yayy?
Retirement's here? Yay?
Retirement? Yay?
Re-tire-ment. Yay.

For the first time in my life I was faced with planning my *own* day and I felt lost. So on Retirement Day 1, when I woke up at 5 AM and didn't have to get up, shower and go to work, I didn't know what to do. Those things that had brought me so much joy for so many years, now seemed to have vanished overnight into an abyss of emptiness. I missed standing in front of a classroom full of eager learners, guiding and inspiring young minds. I missed interacting with colleagues. I missed finding new and refreshing things to do every day.

I muddled through Retirement Day 1, promising myself that Retirement Day 2 would be different. I had planned to start some of the projects I always said I'd do once I "retired," but when I woke up on Retirement Day 2, I couldn't even remember what they were. Even writing had left my mind. Had retirement stricken me with amnesia too? I felt stuck between Scylla and Charybdis. On the one hand, if I did nothing, I'd slip into depression, a pit of pitifulness. Yet, on the other hand, finding something to do was like chasing an elusive butterfly. However, I was determined that retirement would not turn me into a robot of rust like I'd seen it do to so many other seniors. So to jump start my "fun-and-fabulous retirement" I did what I thought most retirees did: I traveled, gardened, made things, did yard work, and ate out. A lot. Fun? Yes. Fulfilling? No. And mixed up in the whole gamut of things was my search for a real church home. I thought that if I could at least satisfy that one area of my life, then the rest would fall into place. I'd been visiting churches for a while but none felt exactly right to me.

Allow me another digression, please. (Bear with me. These digressions are leading you somewhere.)

Just when I felt like I was sinking into an eddy of endless entanglement, God sent me a lifeline in the form of Union Baptist Church. Never in my life had I met such a family of the most welcoming, loving, and giving people. Perfect people? No. But warm, embracing, and caring? A resounding yes! From the first Sunday I attended, I felt the weight of wandering lift from my soul. I was home.

Yes, there have been many changes at Union over the years, but I didn't let those changes chase me away. In fact, I owe that steadfastness to what I learned from my childhood pastor, Reverend W. Odell Howard. Pastor Howard taught his parishioners the difference between joining the church and joining the pastor. He said that if you join the pastor (that is, *because of* the pastor), then when the pastor leaves, you'll leave. But if you join the *church* (that is, a church *family*) no matter how many pastors come and go, you'll still stay. Union is my church *family*, and to me, no church in the world measures up to it. (In fact, I think everyone should feel the same way about *their* church, and if not, then maybe . . ..)

Now back to talking about retirement and those manuscripts, poems, etc. How many digressions ago was it? Do you remember? Oh well, I guess it doesn't matter. Read on, please.

As I said, I thought I'd publish all those manuscripts once I "retired," but the truth is, by the time the dust settled, I'd lost the motivation to submit anything, mainly because I believed my work wasn't worthy of any readership, anyway. No matter how many people complimented me on things I wrote, I still didn't feel accomplished. So I played it safe and wrote only when asked to do so. That included Advent and Lenten devotionals for my church, business letters for people in the community, contracts for my HOA, and so on. I thought all of that would be satisfying, but I was wrong. Nothing could quench the fire that burned inside me. (If only I had remembered Jeremiah 20:9a!)

I would have continued hiding in the background if God hadn't started nudging me again. (Oh Jeremiah, why didn't you tap me on the head with a 2x4 to help me understand?) Actually, I'm grateful for those nudges because they brought to mind several lessons about God's plans for our lives. Lesson One: Our plans are far different from God's plans. (Jer. 29:11) Lesson Two: In any battle – whether of wills, or with human opposition – God will always win. Lesson Three: Our gifts and talents are callings from God, not meant to be hidden from the world nor squandered, but to be treasured and used to help and enlighten others in some way. Finally, Lesson Four: If you don't use your gift, it will consume you.

Number four is how I found my way back. In my wilderness, I had forgotten one simple principle: God cares, and when God wants the best for you, God nudges you toward that ultimate goal.

For me, those little nudges came by way of my pastor's sermons. Periodically, Pastor Rivers preached sermons about not giving up. He told us to keep striving to reach our greatest potential and use the gifts that God had given us. In some sermons, he even said these very words: "There's another book in you." Now how could I have possibly ignored such a direct message from God? Yet I did. I thought to myself, "Surely, God must be speaking to someone else in the church, someone much more prominent and accomplished than I." So I went on with my life, business-as-usual, . . . or so I thought.

It didn't take long for me to figure out that my reluctance to write would not stop the little pokes. Nor would it stop the unextinguishable fire burning within me. (Oh, me, and poor Jeremiah (Jer. 20:9b).

One Sunday morning in January, 2024, during Pastor Rivers' sermon series called "Becoming More," he preached a sermon titled, "You Were Made for More." During that sermon, he said those six, fateful words again: "There's one more book in you." I call them fateful words because on that day, at that moment, something within me shifted. Something miraculous. Something life-changing. I felt new and alive again. It was then that I stopped fighting, stopped holding back, and finally opened my mind to the possibility that there just might be "one more book" in me (or possibly several; who knows but God?).

My immediate impulse was to call the book *One More Book*, but like so many of my impulsive ideas, that one, too, soon faded like a vapor on a hot summer day. The title just didn't quite sit with me. So over the next few months I just focused on writing. In the course of time, my scribe coach and I experimented with several new titles, but when the inspiration came to call it *Truly Grounded: Insights for the Seasons of Life*, that was a hallaluia moment.

Before I end, let me dispel the notion that I had to be pushed – kicking and screaming – into writing again, or that writing is a drudgery and a chore. On the contrary, writing itself is joyful, pleasurable, and enchanting. I love "talking" to you – my audience – as if you are right in front of me. The act of writing definitely is *not* a chore for me. The chore is the four, five, six or more edits that have to be done. Nonetheless, after that Sunday, I promised myself that *this* time things would be different. *This* time I wouldn't quit. *This* time, I would keep writing and submitting until someone "out there" accepted my work. I had lost too much time in self-doubt to stop again.

After that Sunday, when I finally allowed God to use me again, He hit me with another epiphany: Writing (as with other arts) is a gift, and it's one of God's ways of speaking to people. Boom! And there it was, the message that God had probably been trying to get me to see all along. My gift . . . OUR gifts, fellow artists – no matter how small and insignificant we think they are – are meant to be shared. Now I understood why the fire inside me wouldn't stop burning. Writing had less to do with me and more to do with honoring God and helping people. (Did I mention that I'm not the sharpest tool in the toolbox? It takes me a longer to "get it.") I finally realized that I was powerless to stop writing because a writer is who God had created me to be. Why hadn't I seen it before? It was so simple when you think about it. After all, orators have to orate. Builders have to build. Farmers have to farm. Painters have to paint. Teachers have to teach. Eccetera. So writers have to write. Everyone has his or her own, unique gift from God, and we all work together to create this wonderful world where God said, "It is good."

One last thing (well, almost last). I've never written anything merely to make money. I've always written for the pleasure of it and the hope that people would appreciate what I wrote. I confess, though, that part of my reluctance to publish was due to my fear of exposure, as crazy as that sounds. I also feared being brutally honest in my writing. Then I thought of all the writers of the Harlem Renaissance and other years. Did Claude McKay shrink back in fear of writing, *If We Must Die*? Did Langston Hughes shrink back from writing the poem, *Harlem*? Did William Edward Burghardt Du Bois shrink back from writing *The Souls of Black Folk*? And what about James Baldwin, Toni Morrison, Amiri Baraka, Maya Angelou, Alex Haley, and countless other bold writers who chose to express themselves without fear?

I don't think of myself as being in the same category with any of those writers, but one thing became clear to me as I composed *Truy Grounded*. I realized that I must dispel all of my old anxieties about how I would be perceived by others. I realized that I needed to be my true, authentic self and write what I felt, the way I felt it.

And so I write. And so should you, my fellow Divinely inspired and gifted ones. You must write, paint, dance, sing, sew, design, sculpt, speak, photograph, make music, preach, teach, build . . ..

Works Cited

Acocella, Nick. "More Info on Frank Robinson." (July 31, 1973). Special to ESPN.com, Quoting *Time Magazine* (July 31, 1973).   https://www.espn.com/classic/000728 frankrobinsonadd.html.

Albom, Mitch. *The Five People You Meet In Heaven*. Hyperion Publishing, 2003. www.Google.com

Bainbridge, Danielle. "Why Do We Say 'African-American'?" Public Broadcasting Station (PBS). Video. season 3. (Oct. 1, 2020). https://www.pbs.org.

Cooke, Sam. "A Change Is Gonna Come." from *Ain't That Good News*. Album. RCA Victor Records. 1964.

Geisel, Theodor. *Horton Hears a Who*. Random House Publishers. (1954). www.wikipedia.com.

Hall, Will. *9 Life Lessons From Birds*. March 31, 2023. https://birda.org/life-lessons-from-birds/

Hammerstein, II, Oscar. "I Whistle a Happy Tune." from *The King and I*. (1956). Composed by Richard Rodgers. www.wikipedia.com.

Horswood, Geoff, *Grass . . ..* citing Robbins, Kneika, *Serious Thoughts*, (May, 2014). www.WordPress.com (site deleted by the authors).

Jenkins, Stephan, and Cadogan, Kevin. Third Eye Blind. Band (formed in 1993). San Francisco, CA. https://en.wikipedia.org/wiki/Third_Eye_Blind

Jones, Timothy W. (https://www.latrobe.edu. au/news/articles/ 2023/opinion/the-history-of-the-word-queer)

Kahal, Irving & Wheeler, Francis. "Let a Smile Be Your Umbrella." (Dec. 9, 1927). Music composed by Sammy Fain. https://secondhandsongs.com

King, Rodney, "Can we all get along?" https://m.youtube.com/watch?v=1sONfxPCTU0

Little, Malcolm. Phrase "by any means necessary" from *Dirty Hands*. Play by Sartre, Jean-Paul. 1948

LizStoryPlanet. Website blog. *LizStoryPlanet.com*

Morey, Lawrence. "Whistle While You Work." (1937).

Snow White and the Seven Dwarfs? Walt Disney Productions. Music composed by Frank Churchhill. www.wikipedia.com.

Parton, Dolly. "Nine to Five." RCA Nashville Records. Gregg Perry, producer (1980). www.Google.com.

Payne, Thomas. *Common Sense*. Philadelphia, PA. (MDCCLXXVI) (1776). R. Bell Publishers. https://oll.libertyfund.org/pages/1776-paine-common-sense-pamphlet.

- Achieve greatness.
- Press on in the face of adversity.
- Like John Chapman ("Johnny Appleseed") spreading seeds, let us spread love, joy, peace, forbearance, kindness, faithfulness, gentleness, self-control, and more.
- Live, love, and by all means, laugh.
- Take time to hug your children . . . a lot.
- Give what you want to receive. Project what you want to get back.
- Speaking (greeting, saying hello) doesn't cost anything.
- You only know what you know at the time you know it. When you know better you can do better.
- The person whose sentence always begins with "I'm going to . . ." or "I'm about to . . ." never gets anything done.
- The answer to a thousand questions begins by asking the first question.
- Don't give up. It's never over until the "fat lady" sings, and the fat lady is mute.

About The Author

Evelyn Holt-Fuller was born in Mebane, NC. She attended Durham Business College, graduating with a diploma in accounting (Associate Degree equivalency). In 1989, she received a B.A. (cum laude) in English/journalism from North Carolina Central University, where she was a staff editor for Campus Echo. She followed that degree with a Masters of Education degree in 1991. Pursuing her calling to teach, she completed teacher certification in the Program in Education at Duke University in 1995, and was hired immediately by Durham Public Schools (DPS), where she taught standard, Academically Gifted and honors classes. In 2000, she obtained certification in learning disabilities at the University of North Carolina at Chapel Hill, and began teaching in the Exceptional Children's Program of DPS. During her tenure, she became the first coordinator of the inaugural Advancement Via Individual Determination (AVID) program.

Evelyn received many honors and awards in earlier years. She received the Certificate of Merit from North Carolina Central University (1979); the Govenor's Community Service Award (1980); honored with "Evelyn Holt-Fuller Day" while at Glenn Grove UHC; honorable mention, *Law and Contemporary Problems* (Duke Law School scholarly journal) (1993), and *Duke Law Journal* (signed copies of articles written by David Steinberg, 1992 and Reena Glazer, 1993). While employed with Duke Law School as a legal secretary and editorial assistant, she was Editor-in-Chief of

L.A.W. News, a newletter for, and about, the employees
of Duke Law School. She was nominated for Teacher
of the Year, Durham Public Schools (2007) and
received the "Get Involved Initiative," Durham Public
Schools (2012). She is a former member of the Durham
Association of Educators.

Evelyn keeps a library of her published and
unpublished works: *The Harvest Is White* (unpublished
work, 1981); *Kinfolks and Other Unrelated Relatives*
(1993, unpublished); *Don't Mind If I Do: Classroom
Warm-Up Exercises to Sharpen the Mind* (Thomson
Custom Publishing, 2002); *Wisdom and Truth*
(National Poets Anthology, circa 2004); *To My Brown
Babies: A Great-Grandmother's Letter to African-
American Girls and Their Friends* (DogEar Press,
2012); and *JOTS*, originally unpublished until renamed
Truly Grounded: Insights for the Seasons of Life
(2024).

Since 2015, she has been an associate minister at
Union Baptist Church in Durham, North Carolina,
where she serves on the Rest Home Ministry, and is
adjunct teacher of the Sunday School on Wednesday
class.